C000161098

일상 속 진짜 자연스러운 **한국어 대화**
중급

Real-Life Korean Conversations: Intermediate

written by TalkToMeInKorean

Real-Life Korean Conversations: Intermediate

1판 1쇄	1st edition published	2018. 1. 2
1판 7쇄	7th edition published	2021. 6. 21

지은이	Written by	TalkToMeInKorean
책임편집	Edited by	선경화 Kyung-hwa Sun, 에밀리 프리즈러키 Emily Przylucki
디자인	Designed by	선윤아 Yoona Sun
삽화	Illustrations by	까나리 존스 Kanari Jones
녹음	Voice Recordings by	TalkToMeInKorean
펴낸곳	Published by	롱테일북스 Longtail Books
펴낸이	Publisher	이수영 Su Young Lee
편집	Copy-edited by	김보경 Florence Kim
주소	Address	04043 서울 마포구 양화로 12길 16-9(서교동) 북앤빌딩 3층 3rd Floor Book-And Bldg. 16-9 Yanghwa-ro 12-gil, Mapo-gu, Seoul, KOREA
이메일	E-mail	TTMIK@longtailbooks.co.kr
ISBN		979-11-86701-63-8 13710

TTMIK - TALK TO ME IN KOREAN

Real-Life Korean Conversations: Intermediate

일상 속 진짜 자연스러운 **한국어 대화** 중급

Table of Contents

Preface

Learn essential intermediate-level sentence patterns through natural everyday conversations and improve your Korean vocabulary!

This book contains typical Korean dialogues on 30 different topics. They are all very common situations that you may experience in your day-to-day life. The conversations have been written in just the right length for an intermediate learner, and each line has an English translation on the adjacent page. You can listen to every vocabulary word, sample sentence, and complete dialogue from the book using the accompanying audio tracks. You can pick up many useful words in the vocabulary section, and the "Pattern Practice" part in each chapter introduces 3 main grammar patterns or expressions that will help you expand your Korean sentence building skills.

You can study the dialogues from first to last, or choose any topic that interests you and learn the dialogues at your own pace. Thank you for choosing to study with us, and be sure to check out our other books and lessons on our website at TalkToMeInKorean.com!

How to Use This Book

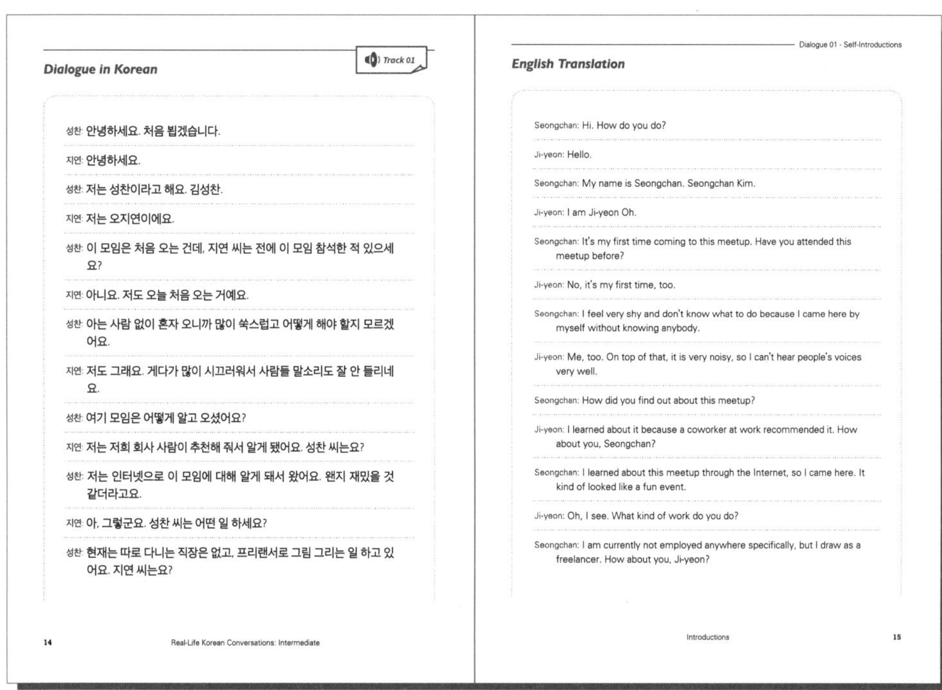

Dialogue in Korean

Track 01

성찬: 안녕하세요. 처음 뵙겠습니다.

지연: 안녕하세요.

성찬: 저는 성찬이라고 해요. 김성찬.

지연: 저는 오지연이에요.

성찬: 이 모임은 처음 오는 건데, 지연 씨는 전에 이 모임 참석한 적 있으세요?

지연: 아니요. 저도 오늘 처음 오는 거예요.

성찬: 아는 사람 없이 혼자 오니까 많이 쑥스럽고 어떻게 해야 할지 모르겠어요.

지연: 저도 그래요. 게다가 많이 시끄러워서 사람들 말소리도 잘 안 들리네요.

성찬: 여기 모임은 어떻게 알고 오셨어요?

지연: 저는 저희 회사 사람이 추천해 줘서 알게 됐어요. 성찬 씨는요?

성찬: 저는 인터넷으로 이 모임에 대해 알게 돼서 왔어요. 왠지 재밌을 것 같더라고요.

지연: 아, 그렇군요. 성찬 씨는 어떤 일 하세요?

성찬: 현재는 따로 다니는 직장은 없고, 프리랜서로 그림 그리는 일 하고 있어요. 지연 씨는요?

14 Real-Life Korean Conversations: Intermediate

Dialogue 01 - Self-Introductions

English Translation

Seongchan: Hi. How do you do?

Ji-yeon: Hello.

Seongchan: My name is Seongchan. Seongchan Kim.

Ji-yeon: I am Ji-yeon Oh.

Seongchan: It's my first time coming to this meetup. Have you attended this meetup before?

Ji-yeon: No, it's my first time, too.

Seongchan: I feel very shy and don't know what to do because I came here by myself without knowing anybody.

Ji-yeon: Me, too. On top of that, it is very noisy, so I can't hear people's voices very well.

Seongchan: How did you find out about this meetup?

Ji-yeon: I learned about it because a coworker at work recommended it. How about you, Seongchan?

Seongchan: I learned about this meetup through the Internet, so I came here. It kind of looked like a fun event.

Ji-yeon: Oh, I see. What kind of work do you do?

Seongchan: I am currently not employed anywhere specifically, but I draw as a freelancer. How about you, Ji-yeon?

Introductions 15

First listen to the dialogue with the audio file provided for free at talktomeinkorean.com/audio. Then, read the Korean conversation on the left side and compare line by line with the English translation on the right side.

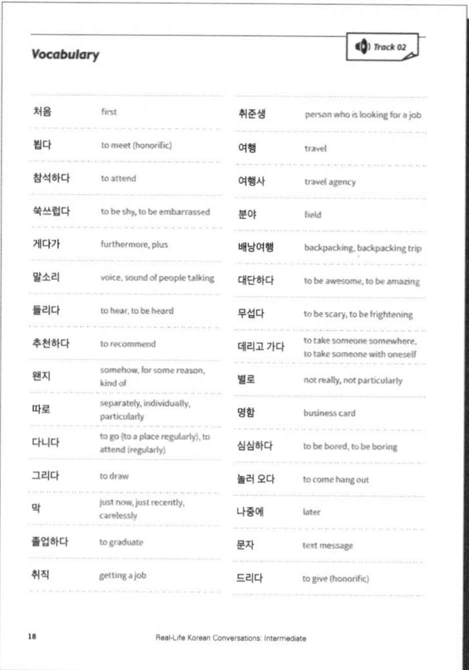

Vocabulary

Track 02

처음	first	취준생	person who is looking for a job
뵙다	to meet (honorific)	여행	travel
참석하다	to attend	여행사	travel agency
쑥쓰럽다	to be shy, to be embarrassed	분야	field
게다가	furthermore, plus	배낭여행	backpacking, backpacking trip
말소리	voice, sound of people talking	대단하다	to be awesome, to be amazing
들리다	to hear, to be heard	무섭다	to be scary, to be frightening
추천하다	to recommend	데리고 가다	to take someone somewhere, to take someone with oneself
왠지	somehow, for some reason, kind of	별로	not really, not particularly
따로	separately, individually, particularly	명함	business card
다니다	to go (to a place regularly), to attend (regularly)	심심하다	to be bored, to be boring
그리다	to draw	놀러 오다	to come hang out
막	just now, just recently, carelessly	나중에	later
졸업하다	to graduate	문자	text message
취직	getting a job	드리다	to give (honorific)

18 Real-Life Korean Conversations: Intermediate

←

*Next, check out the **vocabulary that were used in the dialogue** on the next page.*

You can listen to the pronunciation by a native Korean speaker with the audio file as well.

→

*Study **three grammar patterns** that were used in the dialogue here.*

→

*Take a look at the sentence that was used in the dialogue as well as **two more sample sentences** for each pattern.*

→

***Test yourself** to see if you have fully understood how the pattern works by translating two English sentences.*

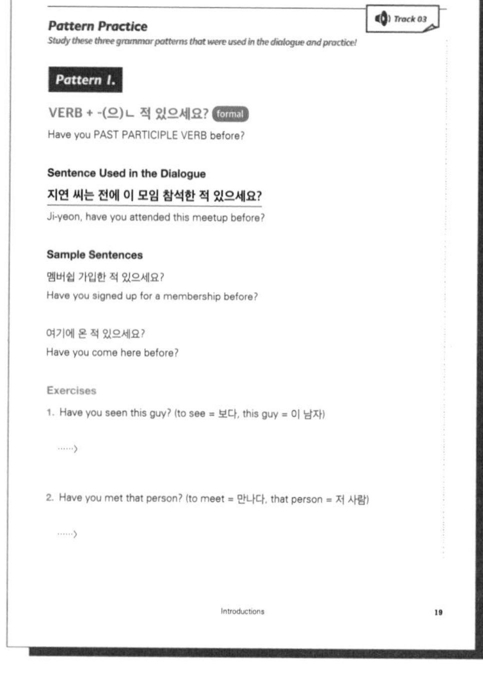

Pattern Practice

Track 03

Study these three grammar patterns that were used in the dialogue and practice!

Pattern 1.

VERB + -(으)ㄴ 적 있으세요? formal

Have you PAST PARTICIPLE VERB before?

Sentence Used in the Dialogue

지연 씨는 전에 이 모임 참석한 적 있으세요?

Ji-yeon, have you attended this meetup before?

Sample Sentences

멤버쉽 가입한 적 있으세요?

Have you signed up for a membership before?

여기에 온 적 있으세요?

Have you come here before?

Exercises

1. Have you seen this guy? (to see = 보다, this guy = 이 남자)

   ......›

2. Have you met that person? (to meet = 만나다, that person = 저 사람)

   ......›

Introductions 19

Answer Key
1. 이 남자 본 적 있으세요? 2. 저 사람 만난 적 있으세요?

Applied Patterns

VERB + -아/어/여 본 적 있어요?

→ 참석해 본 적 있어요?
Have you attended this meetup before?

*Using 있어요? instead of 있으세요? is still formal and polite, but if you do not use -시-, which is the honorific suffix, you will sound a little less formal and more laid back.

VERB + -아/어/여 봤어요?

→ 참석해 봤어요?
Have you attended this meetup before? / Have you tried attending this meet up before?

*-아/어/여 본 적 있어요? would be a more direct translation of "Have you ever PAST PARTICIPLE VERB before?" but you can also say -아/어/여 봤어요? to mean "Have you tried VERB-ing before?"

Pattern 2.

왠지 ADJECTIVE + -(으)ㄹ 것 같더라고요 formal

It kind of looked like it would be ADJECTIVE. / For some reason, I thought it would be ADJECTIVE.

20 Real-Life Korean Conversations: Intermediate

←

You can check out the answers here.

←

The grammar pattern can vary depending on the circumstance or the context. Discover more by looking at the applied patterns here.

You can listen to a native speaker read the sentences with the audio files provided for free at talktomeinkorean.com/audio.

여기 제 명함이에요.

Here's my business card.

Self-Introductions

Dialogue in Korean

성찬: 안녕하세요. 처음 뵙겠습니다.

지연: 안녕하세요.

성찬: 저는 성찬이라고 해요. 김성찬.

지연: 저는 오지연이에요.

성찬: 이 모임은 처음 오는 건데, 지연 씨는 전에 이 모임 참석한 적 있으세요?

지연: 아니요. 저도 오늘 처음 오는 거예요.

성찬: 아는 사람 없이 혼자 오니까 많이 쑥스럽고 어떻게 해야 할지 모르겠어요.

지연: 저도 그래요. 게다가 많이 시끄러워서 사람들 말소리도 잘 안 들리네요.

성찬: 여기 모임은 어떻게 알고 오셨어요?

지연: 저는 저희 회사 사람이 추천해 줘서 알게 됐어요. 성찬 씨는요?

성찬: 저는 인터넷으로 이 모임에 대해 알게 돼서 왔어요. 왠지 재밌을 것 같더라고요.

지연: 아, 그렇군요. 성찬 씨는 어떤 일 하세요?

성찬: 현재는 따로 다니는 직장은 없고, 프리랜서로 그림 그리는 일 하고 있어요. 지연 씨는요?

English Translation

Seongchan: Hi. How do you do?

Ji-yeon: Hello.

Seongchan: My name is Seongchan. Seongchan Kim.

Ji-yeon: I am Ji-yeon Oh.

Seongchan: It's my first time coming to this meetup. Have you attended this meetup before?

Ji-yeon: No, it's my first time, too.

Seongchan: I feel very shy and don't know what to do because I came here by myself without knowing anybody.

Ji-yeon: Me, too. On top of that, it is very noisy, so I can't hear people's voices very well.

Seongchan: How did you find out about this meetup?

Ji-yeon: I learned about it because a coworker at work recommended it. How about you, Seongchan?

Seongchan: I learned about this meetup through the Internet, so I came here. It kind of looked like a fun event.

Ji-yeon: Oh, I see. What kind of work do you do?

Seongchan: I am currently not employed anywhere specifically, but I draw as a freelancer. How about you, Ji-yeon?

지연: 저는 막 졸업해서, 이제 취직 준비하고 있어요.

성찬: 취준생이시군요.

지연: 네. 맞아요.

성찬: 어떤 쪽으로 일을 하고 싶으세요?

지연: 제가 여행을 많이 좋아하거든요. 그래서 여행사에서 일하고 싶어요.

성찬: 좋아하는 분야에서 일하면 정말 좋을 것 같아요. 여행도 자주 하시겠네요?

지연: 많이는 안 해 봤고요. 동남아로 다섯 번 정도 여행 가 봤어요. 그중 한 번은 혼자서 배낭여행으로 가 봤어요.

성찬: 정말 대단하시네요. 저 같으면 무서워서 친구 한 명은 꼭 데리고 갈 것 같은데요.

지연: 사실 별로 무섭지는 않아요. 혼자 여행하면서 느끼고 배울 수 있는 것도 많더라고요. 성찬 씨는 주로 어떤 그림 그리세요?

성찬: 음... 들어오는 일에 따라서 달라요. 여기 제 명함이에요. 심심할 때 사이트 놀러 오시면 제 그림 보실 수 있어요.

지연: 와, 감사합니다. 명함이 참 귀엽네요. 저는 아직 명함 같은 게 없어서... 나중에 문자 하나 드릴게요.

Ji-yeon: I just graduated, so I am preparing to get a job now.

Seongchan: You're looking for a job.

Ji-yeon: Yeah, that's right.

Seongchan: What kind of work do you want to do?

Ji-yeon: I really like traveling. So, I want to work in a travel agency.

Seongchan: It would be great to work in a field that you like. You must travel often, then?

Ji-yeon: I haven't traveled a lot. I've traveled to Southeast Asia about five times. One of those trips was a backpacking trip by myself.

Seongchan: You're so brave! I would be too scared and take a friend with me if I did that.

Ji-yeon: It's not that scary, actually. When you travel alone, there are a lot of things to learn and emotions to feel. What kind of stuff do you usually draw?

Seongchan: Well, it depends on the job that comes in. Here's my business card. If you visit my site when you're not busy, you can see my drawings.

Ji-yeon: Wow, thank you. Your business card design is really cute. I don't have any business cards, so I will send you a text message later.

Vocabulary

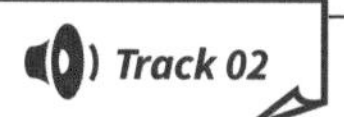

처음	first
뵙다	to meet (honorific)
참석하다	to attend
쑥스럽다	to be shy, to be embarrassed
게다가	furthermore, plus
말소리	voice, sound of people talking
들리다	to hear, to be heard
추천하다	to recommend
왠지	somehow, for some reason, kind of
따로	separately, individually, particularly
다니다	to go (to a place regularly), to attend (regularly)
그리다	to draw
막	just now, just recently, carelessly
졸업하다	to graduate
취직	getting a job
취준생	person who is looking for a job
여행	travel
여행사	travel agency
분야	field
배낭여행	backpacking, backpacking trip
대단하다	to be awesome, to be amazing
무섭다	to be scary, to be frightening
데리고 가다	to take someone somewhere, to take someone with oneself
별로	not really, not particularly
명함	business card
심심하다	to be bored, to be boring
놀러 오다	to come hang out
나중에	later
문자	text message
드리다	to give (honorific)

Pattern Practice

Study these three grammar patterns that were used in the dialogue and practice!

Pattern I.

VERB + -(으)ㄴ 적 있으세요? formal

Have you PAST PARTICIPLE VERB before?

Sentence Used in the Dialogue

지연 씨는 전에 이 모임 참석한 적 있으세요?

Ji-yeon, have you attended this meetup before?

Sample Sentences

멤버쉽 가입한 적 있으세요?

Have you signed up for a membership before?

여기에 온 적 있으세요?

Have you come here before?

Exercises

1. Have you seen this guy before? (to see = 보다, this guy = 이 남자)

   ......〉

2. Have you met that person before? (to meet = 만나다, that person = 저 사람)

   ......〉

Answer Key

1. 이 남자 본 적 있으세요? *2.* 저 사람 만난 적 있으세요?

Applied Patterns

VERB + -아/어/여 본 적 있어요?

→ 참석해 본 적 있어요?

Have you attended before?

*Using 있어요? instead of 있으세요? is still formal and polite, but if you do not use -시-, which is the honorific suffix, you will sound a little less formal and more laid back.

VERB + -아/어/여 봤어요?

→ 참석해 봤어요?

Have you attended before? / Have you tried attending before?

*-아/어/여 본 적 있어요? would be a more direct translation of "Have you ever PAST PARTICIPLE VERB before?" but you can also say -아/어/여 봤어요? to mean "Have you tried VERB-ing before?"

Pattern 2.

왠지 ADJECTIVE + -(으)ㄹ 것 같더라고요 formal

It kind of looked like it would be ADJECTIVE. / For some reason, I thought it would be ADJECTIVE.

Sentence Used in the Dialogue

왠지 재밌을 것 같더라고요.

It kind of looked like it would be fun.

Sample Sentences

왠지 무서울 것 같더라고요.

It kind of looked like it would be scary. / For some reason, I thought it would be scary.

그 영화 왠지 슬플 것 같더라고요.

The movie kind of looked like it would be sad. / For some reason, I thought the movie would be sad.

Exercises

1. It kind of looked delicious. (to be delicious = 맛있다)

   ......〉

2. It kind of looked like it would be okay. (to be okay = 괜찮다)

   ......〉

Answer Key

1. 왠지 맛있을 것 같더라고요. *2.* 왠지 괜찮을 것 같더라고요.

Applied Patterns

왠지 ADJECTIVE + -(으)ㄹ 것 같아 보이더라고요

→ 왠지 재밌을 것 같아 보이더라고요

It kind of seemed like it would be fun.

뭔지 모르게 ADJECTIVE + -(으)ㄹ 것 같더라고요

→ 뭔지 모르게 재밌을 것 같더라고요.

I'm not sure why I thought it, but it seemed like it would be fun.

Pattern 3.

VERB + -(으)시면 VERB + -(으)실 수 있어요 formal

If you VERB, you can VERB.

Sentence Used in the Dialogue

심심할 때 사이트 놀러 오시면 제 그림 보실 수 있어요.

If you visit my site when you're not busy, you can see my drawings.

Sample Sentences

여기로 가시면 나가실 수 있어요.

If you go here, you can go out.

지금 결제하시면 다 보실 수 있어요.

If you pay now, you can watch them all.

Exercises

1. If you wait, you can meet her. (to wait = 기다리다, to meet = 만나다)

······〉

2. If you call now, you can talk to that person. (to call now = 지금 전화하다, to talk to that person = 그 사람과 이야기하다)

······〉

Answer Key

1. 기다리시면 그녀를 만나실 수 있어요. *2.* 지금 전화하시면 그 사람과 이야기하실 수 있어요.

Applied Patterns

VERB + -(으)면 VERB + -(으)ㄹ 수 있어요

→ 사이트 놀러 오면 제 그림 볼 수 있어요.

If you visit my site, you can see my drawings.

*The sentence structure is almost the same, except the honorific suffix -시- has been removed.

만약 VERB + -(으)신다면 VERB + -(으)실 수 있어요

→ 만약 사이트 놀러 오신다면 제 그림 보실 수 있어요.

If you visit my site, you can see my drawings.

*-(으)면 and -(으)ㄴ다면 are very similar, except -(으)ㄴ다면 is more hypothetical than -(으)면.

저도 말씀 많이 들었어요.

I've heard a lot about you, too.

Exchanging Numbers

Dialogue in Korean

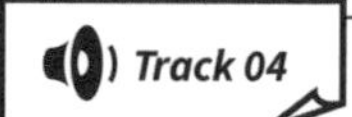

Formal Conversation

미영: 안녕하세요.

수철: 안녕하세요. 처음 뵙겠습니다.

미영: 네, 반갑습니다.

수철: 말씀 많이 들었습니다.

미영: 네. 저도 말씀 많이 들었어요.

수철: 하하. 여기 제 명함입니다.

미영: 아, 네. 감사합니다. 여기 제 명함이에요.

수철: 네, 감사합니다. 날씨가 추워서 오시느라 고생하셨죠?

미영: 아니에요. 지하철역에서 가까워서 금방 찾아왔어요.

수철: 아, 그러셨어요? 식사는 하셨나요?

미영: 네, 방금 하고 왔어요.

수철: 그럼 따뜻한 차라도 한 잔 드릴까요? 녹차? 커피?

미영: 네. 그럼 전 커피 한 잔 주세요.

수철: 네, 알겠습니다. 잠시만요.

미영: 네, 감사합니다.

English Translation

Formal Conversation

Mi-yeong: Hello.

Su-cheol: Hello. How do you do?

Mi-yeong: Nice to meet you.

Su-cheol: I've heard a lot about you.

Mi-yeong: Yeah, I've heard a lot about you, too.

Su-cheol: Haha. Here is my business card.

Mi-yeong: Oh, yes. Thank you. Here is my business card.

Su-cheol: Yes, thank you. It must've been hard to come here because of the cold weather, right?

Mi-yeong: Not at all. It's close to the subway station, so I got here quickly.

Su-cheol: Oh, you did? Did you eat?

Mi-yeong: Yes, I just ate.

Su-cheol: Then would you like some hot tea at least? Green tea? Coffee?

Mi-yeong: Yes. Please give me a cup of coffee then.

Su-cheol: Okay. I got it. Just a second.

Mi-yeong: Thanks.

수철: 여기 있습니다.

미영: 감사합니다.

Casual Conversation

주희: 오빠.

성진: 응.

주희: 우리 다다음 주 수요일 날 발표 아니에요?

성진: 응, 맞아.

주희: 이제 발표 준비 슬슬 해야 하지 않아요?

성진: 응, 이제 준비 시작해야겠다.

주희: 네, 얼른 모여야 할 것 같아요.

성진: 그래. 그럼 이번 주에 팀원들 다 같이 만나서 회의하자.

주희: 네, 그래요.

성진: 그럼 팀원들 다 같이 시간 맞춰 봐야 하니까 단체 채팅방 만들어서 물어볼게.

주희: 네, 좋아요. 오빠 제 번호 있으세요?

성진: 있나? 한번 찾아볼게. 음... 없는 것 같은데... 없다.

Su-cheol: Here you go.

Mi-yeong: Thank you.

Casual Conversation

Ju-hui: Oppa.

Seong-jin: Yeah.

Ju-hui: Aren't we giving a presentation on Wednesday two weeks from now?

Seong-jin: Yes, that's right.

Ju-hui: Shouldn't we start getting ready for the presentation?

Seong-jin: Yeah, I think we'll have to start preparing.

Ju-hui: Yeah, I think we'll have to get together soon.

Seong-jin: Yeah. Alright, let's get together with all the team members this week and have a meeting.

Ju-hui: Okay, let's do that.

Seong-jin: Then, since we have to arrange our schedule to meet all together, I will create a group chat room and ask everyone.

Ju-hui: Yes. That sounds good. Do you have my number?

Seong-jin: Do I? Let me look. Hmm... It looks like I don't have it. I don't have it.

주희: 저도 오빠 번호 없어요.

성진: 서로 번호도 모르고 있었네.

주희: 그러게요. 오빠 번호 뭐예요?

성진: 공일공 일이삼사 일이삼사.

주희: 네. 저장했어요. 제가 전화할게요.

성진: 어, 그래.

성진: 어, 왔어.

주희: 네, 그게 제 번호예요.

성진: 응. 저장할게. 음... 어...

주희: 왜요? 왜 그래요?

성진: 그런데 너... 음... 이름이 뭐였지?

주희: 네?? 하... 정말... 같은 수업을 옆자리 앉아서 몇 개월을 같이 들었는데 어떻게 이름도 몰라요?

성진: 아, 아니야! 내가 모르는 게 아니라, 잠깐 생각이 안 나서 그래. 진짜야.

주희: 제 이름은 '김 같은 수업 옆자리'예요. 너무 길면 그냥 '옆자리'로 저장하세요.

성진: 야! 어디 가? 미안해! 이름은 알려 주고 가! 야, 옆자리!

Ju-hui: I don't have your number either.

Seong-jin: We didn't even know each other's numbers.

Ju-hui: I know, right? What is your number?

Seong-jin: It's 010-1234-1234.

Ju-hui: Okay. I saved it. I will call you.

Seong-jin: Oh, okay.

Seong-jin: Yeah, I got it.

Ju-hui: Yes, that's my number.

Seong-jin: Okay. I'll save it. Um... well...

Ju-hui: Why? What's wrong?

Seong-jin: But what was your name again?

Ju-hui: What? Ha... How... We've been sitting next to each other in the same class for months, and you don't even know my name?

Seong-jin: No. It's not that I don't know. I just can't remember it right now. For real.

Ju-hui: My name is "Person who sits next to me in class Kim". If it's too long, just save it as "Sits next to me".

Seong-jin: Hey, where are you going? I'm sorry. At least let me know your name before you go! Hey! You who sits next to me!

Vocabulary

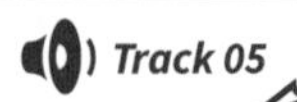

말씀	words (honorific)
날씨	weather
고생하다	to have a hard time, to suffer
지하철역	subway station
가깝다	to be close
식사	meal
방금	just now, a moment ago
차	tea
잔	numerical counter for cups or glasses
녹차	green tea
커피	coffee
다다음 주	the week after next, in two weeks
발표	presentation
준비	preparation
슬슬	slowly, leisurely
모이다	to gather
팀원	team members
회의하다	to have a meeting
맞추다	to adjust
단체	group
채팅방	chat room, group chat
번호	(phone) number
찾아보다	to look for
서로	each other
저장하다	to save
수업	class
옆자리	next seat
잠깐	briefly
길다	to be long
알려주다	to notify

Pattern Practice

Study these three grammar patterns that were used in the dialogue and practice!

Pattern I.

VERB + -아/어/여/야겠다 casual

I think I/we should VERB.

Sentence Used in the Dialogue

이제 준비 시작해야겠다.

I think we should start preparing.

Sample Sentences

지금 전화해 봐야겠다.

I think I should call now.

한 시간 뒤에 출발해야겠다.

I think I should leave in an hour.

Exercises

1. I think I should go get my haircut tomorrow. (to go get one's haircut = 머리 자르러 가다, tomorrow = 내일)

   ······>

2. I think I should bring an umbrella. (to bring = 가지고 가다, umbrella = 우산)

   ······>

Answer Key

1. 내일 머리 자르러 가야겠다. *2.* 우산 가지고 가야겠다.

Applied Patterns

VERB + -아/어/여야 할 것 같아

→ 이제 준비 시작해야 할 것 같아.

It looks like we should start preparing.

VERB + -아/어/여야지

→ 이제 준비 시작해야지.

We should start preparing.

Pattern 2.

어떻게 VERB + -아/어/여요? formal

How could you VERB?

Sentence Used in the Dialogue

어떻게 이름도 몰라요?

How could you not know my name?

Sample Sentences

어떻게 나한테 그래요?

How could you do this to me?

어떻게 우리 기념일을 잊어버려요?

How could you forget our anniversary?

Exercises

1. How could you say something like that? (to say something like that = 그런 말을 하다)

   ……›

2. How could you let something like this pass? (to let something pass = 그냥 넘어 가다)

   ……›

Answer Key

1. 어떻게 그런 말을 해요? *2.* 어떻게 이걸 그냥 넘어가요?

Applied Patterns

어떻게 VERB + -(으)ㄹ 수가 있어요?

→ 어떻게 내 이름도 모를 수가 있어요?

How could you not even know my name?

*어떻게 VERB + -아/어/여요? literally means “How do you VERB?” but it can also mean “How could you VERB?” depending on the context. Whereas, if you say 어떻게 -(으)ㄹ 수가 있어요?, it literally means “How could you even VERB?” and it expresses your surprise or annoyance more.

도대체 어떻게 VERB + -아/어/여요?

→ 도대체 어떻게 내 이름도 몰라요?

How on earth do you not even know my name?

Pattern 3.

VERB/ADJECTIVE + -아/어/여서 그래 casual

It is (SUBJECT does it) because (someone/something) VERB/ADJECTIVE.

Sentence Used in the Dialogue

잠깐 생각이 안 나서 그래.

It is because I just can't remember it right now.

Sample Sentences

그 사람 지금 아파서 그래.

He does that because he is sick now.

다시 만나기 싫어서 그래.

It is because I don't want to see (them) again.

Exercises

1. It is because I am scared. (to be scared = 무섭다)

……›

2. It is because I am sleepy now. (to be sleepy = 졸리다, now = 지금)

······>

Answer Key

1. 무서워서 그래. *2.* 지금 졸려서 그래

Applied Patterns

VERB/ADJECTIVE + -아/어/여서 그래요 formal

→ 잠깐 생각이 안 나서 그래요.

It is because I just can't remember it right now.

VERB/ADJECTIVE + -아/어/여서 그런 거야

→ 잠깐 생각이 안 나서 그런 거야.

It was because I just couldn't remember it for a little while.

*You can use -(으/느)ㄴ 거야 (in casual language) or -(으/느)ㄴ 거예요 (in formal language) when providing some background information or explanation for a certain outcome.

뭐 하고 살아?

What are you up to these days?

•

How are you?

Cas

Dialogue in Korean

수경: 여보세요?

지민: 여보세요? 수경아, 나야!

수경: 누구?

지민: 나 지민이! 핸드폰 번호 바꿨어! 저장해.

수경: 아, 그래? 알겠어.

지민: 요즘 왜 이렇게 조용해? 잘 지내?

수경: 그럼 잘 지내지.

지민: 뭐 하고 살아?

수경: 나야 뭐 그냥 똑같지. 회사, 집, 회사, 집. 너는 어때?

지민: 난 요즘 정신없어. 아, 그리고... 나 곧 결혼해!

수경: 응? 정말? 그때 그 남자랑?

지민: 아, 아니... 그 남자 말고...

수경: 아... 그래? 축하한다, 기집애. 그럼 요즘 많이 바쁘겠구나?

지민: 응, 요즘 결혼 준비하느라 정신이 없어. 미나는 요즘 뭐 한대? 연락해?

English Translation

Su-gyeong: Hello?

Ji-min: Hello? Su-gyeong, it's me!

Su-gyeong: Who?

Ji-min: It's me, Ji-min! I changed my phone number. Save this number.

Su-gyeong: Oh, you did? Okay.

Ji-min: Why have you been so quiet lately? Are you okay?

Su-gyeong: Of course, I'm great.

Ji-min: What are you up to these days?

Su-gyeong: Well, it's the same for me. Work, home, work, home. How about you?

Ji-min: I've been so busy lately. Oh, and I'm getting married soon!

Su-gyeong: What? Really? With that guy from back then?

Ji-min: Oh, no, not that guy.

Su-gyeong: Oh, okay. Congratulations, girl. Then, I guess you must be quite busy lately.

Ji-min: Yeah, I'm quite busy these days with wedding preparations. What is Mina up to these days? Do you keep in touch with her?

수경: 걔도 요즘 연애하느라 바쁘잖아. 연락해 봐!

지민: 아, 그렇구나. 그래야겠다. 조만간 다 같이 한번 보자.

수경: 그래. 한번 뭉치자. 본 지 진짜 오래 됐다.

지민: 그러니깐. 내가 다른 애들한테도 다 연락해 볼게. 만나서 청첩장도 줄겸.

수경: 응. 연락해 보고 나한테도 연락 줘.

지민: 그래 알겠어. 또 연락할게. 잘 지내고 있어.

수경: 응, 그래. 너도! 끊을게.

Su-gyeong: You know these days she's also busy dating. Give her a call!

Ji-min: Oh, I see. I should. Let's meet up all together one of these days.

Su-gyeong: Sure. Let's get together. It's been a really long time since we last met.

Ji-min: Yeah, right. I will call our other friends (in our circle), too. I can give you guys my wedding invitation then as well.

Su-gyeong: Yeah. Call them, and let me know, too.

Ji-min: Okay. I'll call you again. Take care.

Su-gyeong: Alright. You, too! Bye.

Vocabulary

바꾸다	to change
저장하다	to save
요즘	these days
조용하다	to be quiet
똑같다	to be the same
회사	company
집	house
정신없다	to be hectic, to be distracted, to be busy
곧	soon
결혼하다	to marry
남자	man, guy
축하하다	to congratulate
많이	a lot
바쁘다	to be busy
준비하다	to prepare
연락하다	to contact
연애하다	to date, to go out with someone
조만간	sooner or later
같이	together
보다	to see, to watch
뭉치다	to gather
오래	long, for a long time
애들	kids, friends
만나다	to meet
청첩장	wedding invitation
주다	to give
끊다	to hang up

Pattern Practice

Study these three grammar patterns that were used in the dialogue and practice!

Pattern I.

왜 이렇게 ADJECTIVE + -아/어/여? casual

Why am/is/are (SUBJECT) so ADJECTIVE?

Sentence Used in the Dialogue

요즘 왜 이렇게 조용해?

Why are you so quiet lately?

Sample Sentences

저기 왜 이렇게 시끄러워?

Why is it so loud there?

왜 이렇게 비싸?

Why is it so expensive?

Exercises

1. Why is he so handsome? (he/that guy = 저 남자, to be handsome = 잘생기다)

   ......〉

2. Why are you so late? (to be late = 늦다)

   ......〉

Answer Key

1. 저 남자 왜 이렇게 잘생겼어? *2.* 왜 이렇게 늦어?

Applied Patterns

왜 이렇게 ADJECTIVE + -아/어/여요? formal

→ 요즘 왜 이렇게 조용해요?

Why are you so quiet lately?

어째서 이렇게 ADJECTIVE + -아/어/여요? formal

→ 어째서 이렇게 조용해요?

How come you are so quiet lately?

Pattern 2.

VERB + -느라 정신이 없어 casual

(SUBJECT) am/is/are so busy VERB-ing/with NOUN (that SUBJECT am/is/are distracted/feeling stressed)

Sentence Used in the Dialogue

요즘 결혼 준비하느라 정신이 없어.

I'm quite busy these days with wedding preparations.

Sample Sentences

시험 공부하느라 정신이 없어.

I'm so busy studying for my test.

요즘 일하느라 정신이 없어.

I'm so busy with work these days.

Exercises

1. He is so busy dating these days. (He = 그 남자, to date = 연애하다, these days = 요즘)

   ……›

2. They are so busy preparing for the event. (to prepare = 준비하다, the event = 그 행사)

   ……›

Answer Key

1. 그 남자 요즘 연애하느라 정신이 없어. *2.* 그 사람들 그 행사를 준비하느라 정신이 없어.

Applied Patterns

VERB + -느라 정신이 하나도 없어

→ 요즘 결혼 준비하느라 정신이 하나도 없어.

I'm really quite busy these days with wedding preparations.

VERB + -느라 너무 바빠

→ 요즘 결혼 준비하느라 너무 바빠.

I'm too busy preparing for my wedding.

Pattern 3.

VERB + -(으)ㄴ 지 진짜 오래 됐다 casual

It's been so long since (someone/something) last PAST TENSE VERB.

Sentence Used in the Dialogue

본 지 진짜 오래 됐다.

It's been a really long time since we last met.

Sample Sentences

영화관에 온 지 진짜 오래 됐다.

It's been so long since I last went to a theater.

여행간 지 진짜 오래 됐다.

It's been a really long time since I last traveled.

Exercises

1. It's been so long since I last went outside. (to go outside = 밖에 나가다)

   ......〉

2. It's been a really long time since I last took the subway. (to take a subway = 지하철 타다)

   ......〉

Answer Key
1. 밖에 나간 지 진짜 오래 됐다. *2.* 지하철 탄 지 진짜 오래 됐다.

Applied Patterns

VERB + -(으)ㄴ 지 진짜 오래 됐어

→ 본 지 진짜 오래 됐어.
It's been really long since we last met.

*됐다 is an exclamation in the past tense, while 됐어 is in the regular present tense form.

VERB + -(으)ㄴ 지 진짜 오래 된 것 같아

→ 본 지 진짜 오래 된 것 같아.
I think it's been really long since we last met.

우리 일요일에 같이 점심 먹을까?

Do you want to eat lunch together on Sunday?

Plans

Dialogue in Korean

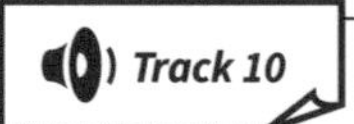

소영: 민주야, 이번 주 토요일에 뭐 해?

민주: 토요일에? 남자 친구 만나.

소영: 남자 친구 주말에 쉬어? 원래 평일에 쉬지 않아?

민주: 응. 근데 이번 주는 주말에 쉴 수 있게 됐어.

소영: 아, 그렇구나. 생일이니까 맛있는 거 먹으러 가겠네.

민주: 응. 안 그래도 지금 맛집 찾아보고 있어.

소영: 어디서 먹을 건데?

민주: 아마 이태원에서?

소영: 그럼 내가 맛집 몇 군데 알려 줄까?

민주: 응. 알려 줘. 알려 줘.

소영: 알겠어. 내가 아예 리스트를 보내 줄게.

민주: 땡큐! 다 니가 직접 가 본 데야?

소영: 당연하지! 내가 맛집을 다 꿰고 있잖아. 일요일에는 뭐 해?

민주: 일요일? 아무것도 안 해.

소영: 그럼 우리 일요일에 같이 점심 먹을까?

English Translation

So-yeong: Minju, what are you doing this Saturday?

Minju: On Saturday? I'm meeting my boyfriend.

So-yeong: Is your boyfriend taking the weekend off? Doesn't he usually have time off during the week?

Minju: Yeah. But this time, he is taking the weekend off.

So-yeong: Oh, I see. Since it's your birthday, I guess you guys will go somewhere to eat something good.

Minju: Yeah. Actually, I was just looking for a nice restaurant now.

So-yeong: Where are you going to eat?

Minju: Probably in Itaewon?

So-yeong: Then do you want me to let you know about a few good places?

Minju: Sure, tell me. Tell me.

So-yeong: Okay. I will just send you a whole list.

Minju: Thanks! Are these all places that you've been to yourself?

So-yeong: Of course! You know that I know nice restaurants like the back of my hand. What are you doing on Sunday?

Minju: Sunday? I'm not doing anything.

So-yeong: Then do you want to eat lunch together on Sunday?

민주: 그래. 상수역?

소영: 콜! 너 생일 선물로 받고 싶은 거 있어?

민주: 글쎄... 갑자기 물어보니까 생각이 안 나네.

소영: 남자 친구는 뭐 사 준대?

민주: 목걸이.

소영: 목걸이? 너 작년에도 남자 친구한테 목걸이 받지 않았어?

민주: 어! 맞아. 기억력 좋네. 나 목걸이 좋아하잖아. 내가 목걸이 사 달라고 했어.

소영: 또 갖고 싶은 거 생각나면 알려 줘.

민주: 아! 생각났어.

소영: 뭔데?

민주: 지갑! 나 진짜 예쁜 지갑 발견했잖아. 잠시만... 이거! 이거 봐 봐!

소영: 우와! 진짜 예쁘다! 근데 너 지갑 바꾼 지 얼마 안 되지 않았어?

민주: 맞아. 근데 이게 너무 예뻐서 갖고 싶어.

소영: 그래. 그럼 그거 생일 선물로 사 줄게.

민주: 오예! 고마워.

Minju: Yeah. Sang-su Station?

So-yeong: Sure! Do you want anything for a birthday present?

Minju: Well, now that you ask me, suddenly I can't think of anything.

So-yeong: What did your boyfriend say he's getting you?

Minju: A necklace.

So-yeong: A necklace? Didn't you receive a necklace from him last year, too?

Minju: Oh, that's right. You have a good memory. You know I like necklaces. I told him to buy me a necklace.

So-yeong: If you think of something else you want, tell me.

Minju: Oh! I remembered.

So-yeong: What is it?

Minju: A wallet. I saw this really pretty wallet. Wait a second... this! Look at this!

So-yeong: Wow! It's so pretty. But, didn't you just get a new wallet a while ago?

Minju: Yes. But this is so pretty, so I want to get it.

So-yeong: Okay, then I will get you that as a birthday present.

Minju: Yes! Thank you.

Vocabulary

이번 주	this week
토요일	Saturday
남자 친구	boyfriend
주말	weekend
쉬다	to rest
평일	weekday
생일	birthday
맛있다	to be tasty
맛집	famous restaurant known for delicious food
찾다	to look for, to search for
아마	probably, perhaps
군데	place, spot
알려 주다	to let someone know
보내 주다	to send
직접	in person
당연하다	to be natural, to be reasonable
꿰고 있다	to know really well, to be very knowledgeable about something
점심	lunch
생일	birthday
선물	gift, present
갑자기	suddenly
물어보다	to ask
목걸이	necklace
작년	last year
기억력	memory
지갑	wallet
발견하다	to discover
바꾸다	to change
갖다	to have
사 주다	to buy someone something

Pattern Practice

Study these three grammar patterns that were used in the dialogue and practice!

Pattern 1.

VERB/ADJECTIVE + -게 됐어 casual

(SUBJECT) happened to VERB... / (SUBJECT) somehow ended up VERB-ing...

Sentence Used in the Dialogue

이번 주는 주말에 쉴 수 있게 됐어.

He happened to be able to take this weekend off.

Sample Sentences

어쩔 수 없이 번호를 바꾸게 됐어.

I ended up having to change my number.

어쩌다 보니 그렇게 됐어.

The situation ended up being like that.

Exercises

1. I happened to be put in charge of that task. (to be put in charge of = 맡게 되다, that task = 그 일)

   ......〉

2. I happened to see him at a café. (to see = 보다, at a café = 카페에서)

   ......〉

Answer Key

1. 그 일을 내가 맡게 됐어. 2. 그 사람을 카페에서 보게 됐어.

Applied Patterns

어쩌다 보니 VERB/ADJECTIVE + -게 됐어

→ 어쩌다 보니 이번 주는 주말에 쉴 수 있게 됐어.

Somehow I happened to be able to take this weekend off.

*어쩌다 보니 is short for 어떻게 하다 보니 and it means that "somehow" something has come to occur, and it is used when you want to emphasize that it was a coincidence.

VERB/ADJECTIVE + -게 됐어요 formal

→ 이번 주는 주말에 쉴 수 있게 됐어요.

I happened to be able to take this weekend off.

Pattern 2.

VERB + -고 있어 casual

(SUBJECT) am/is/are VERB-ing.

Sentence Used in the Dialogue

지금 맛집 찾아보고 있어.

I'm looking for a nice restaurant now.

Sample Sentences

지금 저녁 먹고 있어.

I'm eating dinner now.

그 사람 일하고 있어.
He is working now.

Exercises

1. I'm drinking now. (to drink = 술 마시다, now = 지금)

   ······›

2. My friends are coming now. (my friends = 내 친구들, to come = 오다, now = 지금)

   ······›

Answer Key
1. 지금 술 마시고 있어. *2.* 내 친구들 지금 오고 있어.

Applied Patterns

VERB + -는 중이야

→ 지금 맛집 찾아보는 중이야.
I'm in the middle of looking for a nice restaurant now.

VERB + -고 계셔

→ 지금 맛집 찾아보고 계셔.
They are looking for a nice restaurant now.

*계시다 is an honorific version of 있다. If you are talking to someone older than you or in a higher position than you ABOUT an older or higher-up person, you use 계셔요. If you are talking to your close friends ABOUT an older or higher-up person, you can say 계셔.

Pattern 3.

우리 같이 VERB + -(으)ㄹ까? casual

Shall we VERB together?

Sentence Used in the Dialogue

우리 일요일에 같이 점심 먹을까?

Shall we eat lunch together on Sunday?

Sample Sentences

우리 오늘 같이 야구 보러 갈까?

Shall we go watch a baseball game today?

우리 저녁에 삼겹살 먹을까?

Shall we eat sam-gyeop-sal for dinner?

Exercises

1. Shall we watch a movie together tonight? (we = 우리, to watch = 보다, a movie = 그 영화, tonight = 오늘 저녁에)

……›

2. Shall we go to the park together this weekend? (to go = 가다, park = 공원, this weekend = 이번 주말에)

······〉

Answer Key

1. 우리 오늘 저녁에 같이 그 영화 볼까? *2.* 우리 이번 주말에 같이 공원 갈까?

Applied Patterns

우리 VERB + -(으)ㄹ까?

→ 우리 일요일에 점심 먹을까?

Shall we have lunch on Sunday?

우리 같이 VERB + -(으)ㄹ래?

→ 우리 일요일에 같이 점심 먹을래?

Do you want to have lunch together on Sunday?

이번 크리스마스 계획 있어?

Do you have plans for this Christmas?

•

Dinner

Dialogue in Korean

은진: 소영아, 이번 크리스마스 계획 있어?

소영: 아니, 아직 아무 계획도 없어. 너는?

은진: 우리도 아무 계획이 없어서, 신랑이랑 얘기했는데, 친한 사람들 초대해서 우리 집에서 간단하게 식사하면서 술 마시면 어떨까 해.

소영: 진짜? 그럼 정말 좋지. 그런 날은 밖에 나가도 사람 너무 많아서 싫더라. 음식이랑 다 몇 배로 비싸지고. 우리도 조용히 보내고 싶었는데 막상 집에만 있자니 아쉽더라고.

은진: 잘됐다. 은경이네도 같이 보자. 은경이 남자 친구도 보고 싶고.

소영: 은경이도 아직 계획 없으려나? 같이 보면 좋지. 힘드니까 음식 같은 거 하지 말고 시켜 먹거나 사다 먹을까?

은진: 음, 우선 우리가 음식 조금 하고, 부족하면 시켜 먹거나 하자.

소영: 안 힘들겠어?

은진: 괜찮아. 해 먹는 재미도 있지, 뭐. 근데 막 예쁘게 꾸미거나 하지는 못한다?

소영: 에이. 그런 거 다 필요 없어. 그냥 같이 모여서 먹고 마시는 게 좋은 거지.

English Translation

Eunjin: Soyeong, do you have plans for this Christmas?

Soyeong: No, I don't have any plans yet. How about you?

Eunjin: We don't have any plans, either. I was talking with my husband, and we are thinking of inviting some close friends over and having a simple meal and drinks at our place.

Soyeong: Really? That would be great. On such a day (Christmas), even if you go out, there are too many people, so I don't like that. Food and everything becomes much more expensive. We also wanted to spend the holiday quietly, but I felt like something was missing when we actually decided to stay at home.

Eunjin: That's true. Let's also meet with Eunkyeong's family. I also want to meet her boyfriend.

Soyeong: Eunkyeong probably doesn't have plans yet either, right? It will be great to meet up together. Don't cook because it'll be too much work. How about we just order delivery or buy food?

Eunjin: Hmm, we can cook a little bit of food first, and if it's not enough, let's order delivery or something.

Soyeong: You sure it won't be too much work for you?

Eunjin: It's okay. It's fun to cook. But I can't decorate the food in a pretty way or anything, is that okay?

Soyeong: Come on. That's not necessary. It's just good to get together, eat, and drink.

은진: 그래그래. 술은 얼마나 사지?

소영: 글쎄, 남자들이 술을 얼마나 마실지 모르겠네.

은진: 은경이 남자 친구 술 잘 마신다고 했었어. 그건 은경이한테 물어봐야겠다.

소영: 그래. 은경이도 좋아할 거야. 우리는 뭐 사 갈까? 필요한 거 없어?

은진: 없어. 없어. 그냥 와.

소영: 음... 그럼 우리 회비를 걷자. 그게 서로 부담도 안 될 거 같아.

은진: 그래? 음... 그래, 그러자.

소영: 이번에 니네 집에서 놀고, 다음에 우리 집에서 모이고 하면 되잖아.

은진: 좋아.

Eunjin: You're right. How much alcohol should we buy?

Soyeong: Well, I don't know how much alcohol the guys will drink.

Eunjin: I heard that Eunkyeong's boyfriend can drink a lot. Let me ask Eunkyeong.

Soyeong: Okay. I think Eunkyeong will like it, too. What shall we bring? Do you need anything?

Eunjin: Nothing. Just bring yourselves.

Soyeong: Hmm... then let's pool our money. That way, it won't be a burden on any of us.

Eunjin: Really? Well, okay. Let's do that.

Soyeong: We can hang out at your place this time, and we can get together at our place next time.

Eunjin: Sounds good.

Vocabulary

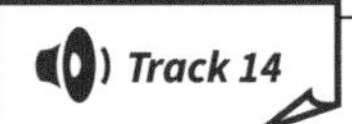

계획	plan
신랑	groom, husband
얘기하다	to talk
친하다	to be close
초대하다	to invite
간단하게	simply, briefly
술	alcohol
마시다	to drink
밖	outside
나가다	to go out
싫다	to hate, to dislike
음식	food
배	multiple, times
비싸다	to be expensive
조용히	quietly
보내다	to spend
-만	only
아쉽다	to be such a pity
힘들다	to be difficult, to be tough, to be hard
시켜 먹다	to order food for delivery and eat it
사다 먹다	to buy some food and eat it
우선	firstly, first of all
조금	a little bit
부족하다	to be insufficient, to be not enough, to lack
재미	fun, interesting
꾸미다	to decorate
필요	need
회비	membership fee, a pool of money
부담	burden
놀다	to hang out

Pattern Practice

Study these three grammar patterns that were used in the dialogue and practice!

Pattern 1.

아무 NOUN + -도 없어 casual

There isn't/aren't any NOUN.

Sentence Used in the Dialogue

아무 계획도 없어.

We don't have any plans.

Sample Sentences

아무 조건도 없어.

There aren't any conditions.

여기 아무 것도 없어.

There is nothing here.

Exercises

1. There has been no word. (word = 말)

    ······〉

2. There isn't any special occasion. (any special occasion = 일)

    ······〉

Answer Key

1. 아무 말도 없어. 2. 아무 일도 없어.

Applied Patterns

아무런 NOUN + -도 없어

→ 아무런 계획도 없어.

We don't have any plans.

*아무 and 아무런 are very similar, but 아무런 emphasizes the meaning of "nothing at all".

전혀 NOUN + -이/가 없어

→ 전혀 계획이 없어.

We have no plans at all.

Pattern 2.

같이 VERB + -자 casual

Let's VERB together.

Sentence Used in the Dialogue

은경이네도 같이 보자.

Let's also meet with Eunkyeong's family.

Sample Sentences

같이 영화 보자.

Let's watch a movie together.

오늘 밤에 같이 놀자.

Let's hang out together tonight.

Exercises

1. Let's eat together. (to eat = 먹다)

    ······>

2. Let's listen to the song together. (to listen to the song = 노래 듣다)

    ······>

Answer Key

1. 같이 먹자. *2.* 노래 같이 듣자

Applied Patterns

같이 VERB + -(으)ㄹ래?

→ 은경이네도 같이 볼래?

Shall we also meet Eunkyeong's family?

VERB + -자

→ 은경이네도 보자.

Let's also meet with Eunkyeong's family.

*Since you are already discussing plans with the listener, the meaning of the sentence doesn't change much even without the word 같이.

Pattern 3.

(Someone/Something) + (-이/가) 얼마나 VERB/ ADJECTIVE + -(으)ㄹ지 모르겠네 casual

I don't know how (much/many/ADJECTIVE) (someone/something) will VERB/be.

Sentence Used in the Dialogue

남자들이 술을 얼마나 마실지 모르겠네.

I don't know how much alcohol the guys will drink.

Sample Sentences

사람들이 얼마나 올지 모르겠네.

I don't know how many people will come.

얼마나 걸릴지 모르겠네.

I don't know how long it will take.

Exercises

1. I don't know how late they will be. (to be late = 늦다, they = 그 사람들)

   ......>

2. I don't know how much he will eat. (he = 그 남자, to eat = 먹다)

   ......>

Answer Key
1. 그 사람들이 얼마나 늦을지 모르겠네. *2*. 그 남자가 얼마나 먹을지 모르겠네.

Applied Patterns

(Someone/Something) + (-이/가) 얼마나 VERB/ADJECTIVE + -(으)ㄹ지 모르겠어

→ 남자들이 술을 얼마나 마실지 모르겠어.
I don't know how much alcohol the guys will drink.

*The original sentence in the dialogue, 모르겠네 uses -네 for the ending to show that a person realizes and acknowledges that they don't know something, whereas 모르겠어 is a more just saying that you don't know something.

(Someone/Something) + (-이/가) 얼마나 VERB/ADJECTIVE + -았/었/였는지 모르겠네

→ 남자들이 술을 얼마나 마셨는지 모르겠네.
I don't know how much alcohol the guys drank.

나 결혼해.

I'm getting married.

Wedding

Dialogue in Korean

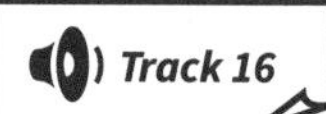

수정: 영진아, 다음 달 말에 혹시 시간 있어?

영진: 글쎄, 잘 모르겠는데. 무슨 일 있어?

수정: 아, 나 결혼해.

영진: 우와, 진짜? 결국 가는구나. 야, 난 너 못 갈 줄 알았어.

수정: 짚신도 짝이 있다고 하잖아.

영진: 그래. 아무튼, 지금 한창 바쁘겠다. 그치?

수정: 말도 마. 드레스 고르고, 스튜디오 촬영하고, 결혼식장 찾으러 돌아다니고... 몸이 열 개였으면 좋겠어.

영진: 그럼 전에 술자리에서 본 그 사람이랑 결혼하는 거야?

수정: 누구? 아, 승재 씨?

영진: 응. 안경 끼고 키 컸던 그분.

수정: 아니야. 다른 사람이랑 결혼해. 승재 씨랑 헤어진 지 꽤 됐어.

영진: 그렇구나. 결혼할 사람은 괜찮은 사람이야?

수정: 응. 말도 잘 통하고, 착하고, 듬직해.

영진: 그래. 잘 됐다. 결혼식은 언제 하는데?

English Translation

Sujeong: Yeong-jin, by any chance do you have some time at the end of next month?

Yeong-jin: Well, I'm not sure. What's up?

Sujeong: Well, I'm getting married.

Yeong-jin: Wow, really? You're finally getting married. I didn't think that you would get married.

Sujeong: They say every Jack has a Jill.

Yeong-jin: Yeah. Anyway, you must be quite busy these days, right?

Sujeong: Tell me about it. Choosing dresses, going to a studio to have our photos taken, and searching for a wedding hall... I wish I had ten bodies.

Yeong-jin: Then, are you getting married to the guy I saw at the party before?

Sujeong: Who? Oh, Seung-jae?

Yeong-jin: Yeah. The tall guy with glasses.

Sujeong: No. I'm marrying someone else. It's been a while since I broke up with Seung-jae.

Yeong-jin: I see. The guy you are marrying, is he a good guy?

Sujeong: Yeah. We understand each other well, and he's nice and reliable.

Yeong-jin: Oh, great to hear that! When is the wedding ceremony?

수정: 다음 달, 20일이야. 청첩장은 모바일로 보내도 되지?

영진: 응. 모바일로 보내 줘.

수정: 우리 학교 다닐 때 같이 알던 친구들 있으면 같이 데리고 와.

영진: 응. 우리 동아리 같이 했던 애들한테도 알려 줄게. 아, 병주도 데리고 갈게.

수정: 야, 죽을래? 병주랑 나랑 사이 안 좋은 거 알잖아.

영진: 너네 둘이 싸워서? 그거 완전 옛날 일 아니야? 다 지난 일인데 뭐 어때? 한때는 같이 잘 지냈잖아.

수정: 아니야, 병주 보면 좀 불편할 것 같아. 걔는 데려오지 마.

영진: 알았어.

수정: 절대 데려오면 안 된다! 알았지? 어?

Sujeong: Next month, on the 20th. It's okay to send you a mobile wedding invitation, right?

Yeong-jin: Yeah, send it via mobile.

Sujeong: If you still know any of our friends who we used to know together back in school, please bring them, too.

Yeong-jin: Yeah. I will let the members of our college club know as well. Oh, I'll bring Byeong-ju, too.

Sujeong: Hey, are you kidding me? You know Byeong-ju and I are not getting along.

Yeong-jin: Because you guys had a fight? Wasn't that a really long time ago? What harm could it do? It's in the past. You used to get along once.

Sujeong: No, I think I'll be a bit uncomfortable seeing him. Don't bring him.

Yeong-jin: Okay.

Sujeong: You can never bring him, okay?

Vocabulary

Track 17

혹시	by any chance
결혼하다	to marry
결국	finally, in the end
짚신	straw shoes
짝	pair
한창	peak, climax
드레스	dress
고르다	to pick, to choose
촬영하다	to film
결혼식장	wedding hall
돌아다니다	to go around, to wander around
술자리	drinking occasion, party with drinks
끼다	to wear (glasses)
헤어지다	to break up
꽤	pretty, quite, very
말이 잘 통하다	to connect well with each other, to understand each other well
착하다	to be nice, to be good-hearted
듬직하다	to be reliable, to be dependable
결혼식	wedding ceremony
청첩장	wedding invitation
동아리	school club
데리고 가다	to take someone somewhere, to take someone with oneself
사이	relationship, relations
싸우다	to fight, to argue
옛날	the old days, past
지난	past, last
한때	for a while, in the past
잘 지내다	to get along with
불편하다	to be uncomfortable
데려오다	to bring

Track 18

Pattern Practice

Study these three grammar patterns that were used in the dialogue and practice!

Pattern I.

혹시 NOUN 있어? casual

Do you have NOUN by any chance?

Sentence Used in the Dialogue

혹시 시간 있어?

Do you have some time by any chance?

Sample Sentences

혹시 연필 있어?

Do you have a pencil by any chance?

혹시 남자 친구 있어?

Do you have a boyfriend by any chance?

Exercises

1. Do you have a different color by any chance? (a different color = 다른 색깔)

   ······〉

2. Do you have more of this by any chance? (more of this = 이거 더)

   ······〉

Answer Key

1. 혹시 다른 색깔 있어? *2.* 혹시 이거 더 있어?

Applied Patterns

혹시 NOUN 있으세요? formal

→ 혹시 시간 있으세요?

Do you have some time by any chance?

혹시 NOUN 있나요? formal

→ 혹시 시간 있나요?

I wonder if you have some time by any chance?

Pattern 2.

난 (someone) + (-이/가) 못 VERB + -(으)ㄹ 줄 알았어 casual

I didn't think (someone) would be able to VERB.

Sentence Used in the Dialogue

난 너 못 갈 줄 알았어.

I didn't think you would be able to go.

Sample Sentences

난 네가 못 할 줄 알았어.

I didn't think you would be able to do it.

난 이거 못 먹을 줄 알았어.

I didn't think I would be able to eat this.

Exercises

1. I didn't think I would be able to finish this today. (to finish = 끝내다)

   ......〉

2. I didn't think we would be able to meet again. (we = 우리, to meet = 만나다, again = 다시)

   ......〉

Answer Key

1. 난 이거 오늘 못 끝낼 줄 알았어. *2.* 난 우리(가) 다시 못 만날 줄 알았어.

Applied Patterns

난 (someone) + (-이/가) VERB + -(으)ㄹ 줄 몰랐어

→ 난 네가 갈 줄 몰랐어.

I didn't know you would go.

난 (someone) + (-이/가) 못 VERB + -(으)ㄹ 줄 알았는데

→ 난 네가 못 갈 줄 알았는데.

I thought you wouldn't be able to go.

Pattern 3.

VERB + -아/어/여도 되지? casual

It's okay to VERB, right?

Sentence Used in the Dialogue

청첩장 모바일로 보내도 되지?

It's okay to send my wedding invitation to your mobile phone, right?

Sample Sentences

나 들어가도 되지?

I can come in, right?

나 이거 먹어도 되지?

I can eat this, right?

Exercises

1. It's okay to use this, right? (to use = 쓰다, this = 이거)

   ......〉

2. It's okay for us to start first, right? (us = 우리, to start = 시작하다, first = 먼저)

   ......〉

Answer Key
1. 나 이거 써도 되지? *2.* 우리 먼저 시작해도 되지?

Applied Patterns

VERB + -아/어/여도 되는 거지?

→ 청첩장 모바일로 보내도 되는 거지?
It's okay to send my wedding invitation to your mobile phone, right?

*Instead of saying 되지?, you can also say 되는 거지? to make the sentence slightly less direct and a little softer.

VERB + -아/어/여도 되죠? formal

→ 청첩장 모바일로 보내도 되죠?
It's okay to send my wedding invitation to your mobile phone, right?

오늘도 늦어?

Are you going to be late again today?

Coming Home

Dialogue in Korean

엄마: 아인아, 오늘 몇 시에 들어와? 오늘도 늦어?

아인: 왜요? 오늘도 늦을 거 같은데. 저 요즘 학교에서 팀별로 하는 프로젝트가 있거든요.

혜영: 엄마, 믿지 마. 오빠 어제도 술 마시고 왔어. 술 냄새 엄청 많이 나더라고.

아인: 프로젝트 준비 끝나고 같이 술 한잔한 거지. 이거 엄청 중요한 프로젝트라서 어쩔 수 없어.

엄마: 아영이는 오늘 몇 시에 들어오는데?

아영: 난 일찍 올 거야. 회사 끝나고 바로 올 거 같아.

엄마: 넌 데이트도 없니? 남자 친구도 좀 사귀고 그래야지.

아영: 오빠한테는 일찍 들어오라고 그러면서 나한테는 왜 늦게 오래? 아, 몰라. 요즘 회사에서 피곤해. 데이트 같은 거 할 시간도 없어.

엄마: 엄마 아는 사람이 소개팅 시켜 준다고 하는데 한번 해 볼래?

혜영: 엄마, 내가 할까? 나도 남자 친구 없는데.

엄마: 아영아, 이번에는 조건도 아주 좋아. 키도 크고 얼굴도 잘생겼대.

아영: 안 해. 저번에도 잘생겼다고 해서 나갔더니 완전 폭탄이었으면서. 엄마 말 이제 안 믿어.

엄마: 알았어. 다른 집 딸들은 남자 친구 생겼다고 소개도 시켜 준다고 하더라.

English Translation

Mother: A-in, what time are you coming home today? Are you going to be late again?

A-in: Why? I think I'll be late again. These days I have a team project at school.

Hye-yeong: Mom, don't believe him. He came home drunk again last night. I smelled so much alcohol on his breath.

A-in: We had a little drink together after the project preparation finished. It's a very important project, so we had no choice.

Mother: A-yeong, what time are you coming home?

A-yeong: I'm coming home early. I think I'll come back right after work finishes.

Mother: Don't you have any dates to go on? You need to get a boyfriend, too.

A-yeong: Why do you tell oppa to come home early but tell me to come home late? Gosh. I'm so tired at work these days. I don't have time for dating.

Mother: My friend wants to set you up with someone. Do you want to try meeting him?

Hye-yeong: Mom, shall I do it instead? I don't have a boyfriend, either.

Mother: A-yeong, this time, the man has some good qualities. I heard he's tall and handsome, too.

A-yeong: No. You told me last time that the guy was handsome, so I went, and he was a complete disaster. I don't believe you anymore.

Mother: Alright. My friends say their daughters introduce their new boyfriends to them.

아영: 엄마, 나 나가요. 나 요즘 회사에서 피곤해서 집에 와서도 아무것도 못하고 잠만 자잖아. 퇴근하고 바로 들어올게요.

엄마: 알았어. 고생해라. 그리고 혜영아, 여기 도시락. 넌 학교 끝나고 바로 올 거지?

혜영: 엄마, 나도 오늘 늦어.

엄마: 뭐? 너 시험이 내일모레인데 왜 늦어? 오늘 늦기만 해 봐.

혜영: 언니한테는 늦어도 된다고 하고, 난 왜 안 되는데?

엄마: 넌 고등학생이잖아. 너도 대학 가서 실컷 놀아. 너 시험 망치기만 해 봐. 엄마한테 혼날 줄 알아.

혜영: 아, 맨날 공부 공부 공부! 나도 피곤하다고! 다녀올게요.

엄마: 혜영아, 도시락 가져가야지.

아인: 나도 갔다 올게, 엄마. 나 12시 넘어서 들어올 거니까 기다리지 말고 그냥 주무세요.

엄마: 알았어. 저녁 잘 먹고 다녀.

아빠: 여보, 난 오늘 야근 없어요. 일찍 들어올 거야.

엄마: 네? 진짜요? 회사에서 저녁 먹고 들어오면 안 돼요?

아빠: 응?

엄마: 아휴, 아니에요. 알겠어요. 늦겠어요. 빨리 출근해요.

A-yeong: Mom, I'm heading out. You know I'm tired at work these days and can't do anything but just sleep. I'll come back home right after work.

Mother: Alright. Have a good day. And Hye-yeong, here's your lunch box. You're coming back right after school, right?

Hye-yeong: Mom, I'll be late, too.

Mother: What? You have an exam coming up in a couple of days. Why will you be late? Don't you dare come home late today.

Hye-yeong: You tell eonni it's okay to be late, but why not me?

Mother: You are a high school student. When you go to college you can have all the fun you want. Screw up this exam, and you will be in trouble.

Hye-yeong: It's always study, study, study! I'm tired, too! See you.

Mother: Hye-yeong, you should take your lunch box.

A-in: I'm heading out too, Mom. I will come home past midnight, so please don't wait and just go to bed.

Mother: Okay. Make sure you have a proper dinner, too.

Father: Honey, I don't have to work overtime. I'll be coming home early.

Mother: What? Really? Can't you eat at the office before you come home?

Father: Huh?

Mother: Well, forget it. I got it. You'll be late. Hurry up and go to work.

Vocabulary

늦다	to be late
팀별	team, divided by teams
믿다	to believe
냄새나다	to smell
엄청나게	tremendously, very
준비	preparation
끝나다	to finish
중요하다	to be important
어쩔 수 없다	to have no choice
바로	straight, directly
남자 친구	boyfriend
사귀다	to date, to go out with
피곤하다	to be tired
소개팅	blind date
시켜 주다	to let someone do something
조건	condition
키가 크다	to be tall
잘생기다	to be handsome, to be good-looking
폭탄	(slang) bomb, dud, disaster
믿다	to believe
퇴근	leaving work
고생하다	to have a hard time, to suffer
실컷	as much as one likes
놀다	to hang out, to play
망치다	to screw up
혼나다	to get a scolding, to be scolded
주무시다	to sleep (honorific)
야근	working overtime
빨리	quickly
출근하다	to go to work

Pattern Practice

Study these three grammar patterns that were used in the dialogue and practice!

Pattern I.

NOUN + -(이)라서 어쩔 수 없어 casual

I/We have no choice because it is NOUN. / I/We can't help it because it is NOUN.

Sentence Used in the Dialogue

이거 엄청 중요한 프로젝트라서 어쩔 수 없어.

It's a very important project, so we have no choice.

Sample Sentences

이게 마지막이라서 어쩔 수 없어.

I have no choice because it is the last one.

내 것이 아니라서 어쩔 수 없어.

I really can't because it is not mine.

Exercises

1. I can't help it because it is tomorrow. (tomorrow = 내일)

······>

2. I have no choice because she is a baby. (baby = 아기)

······>

Answer Key

1. 내일이라서 어쩔 수 없어. *2.* 아기라서 어쩔 수 없어.

Applied Patterns

NOUN + -(이)기 때문에 어쩔 수 없어

→ 이거 엄청 중요한 프로젝트기 때문에 어쩔 수 없어.

Because it's a very important project, we have no choice.

NOUN + -(이)라 어쩔 수 없어

→ 이거 엄청 중요한 프로젝트라 어쩔 수 없어.

It's a very important project, so we have no choice.

*-(이)라 is a shorter form than -(이)라서 but it means exactly the same thing.

Pattern 2.

VERB + -기만 해 봐 casual

Don't you dare VERB. / You'll be in big trouble if you VERB.

Sentence Used in the Dialogue

오늘 늦기만 해 봐.

Don't you dare be late today.

Sample Sentences

이거 먹기만 해 봐.

Don't you dare eat this.

먼저 시작하기만 해 봐.

Don't you dare start first.

Exercises

1. Don't you dare meet that girl. (to meet = 만나다, that girl = 그 여자)

 ……〉

2. You'll be in big trouble if you don't show up today. (to not show up = 안 나타나다, today = 오늘)

 ……〉

Answer Key

1. 그 여자 만나기만 해 봐. *2.* 오늘 안 나타나기만 해 봐.

Applied Patterns

VERB + -기만 해 봐라

→ 오늘 늦기만 해 봐라.

Don't you dare be late today.

*The -라 ending is used in commands, and combined with -해 봐, it makes your sentence sound slightly more threatening.

VERB + -(으)면 가만 안 있어

→ 오늘 늦으면 가만 안 있어.

If you are late today, I won't let it pass.

Pattern 3.

VERB + -(으)면 안 돼요? formal

Couldn't you (just) VERB?

Sentence Used in the Dialogue

회사에서 저녁 먹고 들어오면 안 돼요?

Couldn't you (just) eat at the office before you come home?

Sample Sentences

이거 오늘 끝내면 안 돼요?

Couldn't you (just) finish this today?

이 영화 그만 보면 안 돼요?

Couldn't you (just) stop watching this movie?

Exercises

1. Couldn't you (just) stop talking? (to stop talking = 그만 말하다)

   ......〉

2. Couldn't you (just) do it for me? (to do it for me = 날 위해 해 주다)

   ......〉

Answer Key
1. 그만 말하면 안 돼요? *2.* 날 위해 해 주면 안 돼요?

Applied Patterns

VERB + -(으)면 안 될까요?

→ 회사에서 저녁 먹고 들어오면 안 될까요?
Can't you eat at the office before you come home?

*안 돼요? is a more direct way of asking "can't you?" whereas by saying 안 될까요?, you are not only asking the other person but you also sound like you are wondering about it out loud.

VERB + -(으)면 안 되겠죠?

→ 회사에서 저녁 먹고 들어오면 안 되겠죠?
You can't eat at the office before you come home, right?

저 내일 여섯 시에 깨워 주세요.

Please wake me up at 6 o'clock tomorrow.

Waking Up

Dialogue in Korean

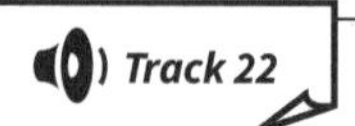

철수: 엄마. 저 내일 여섯 시에 깨워 주세요.

엄마: 여섯 시? 아침 여섯 시?

철수: 네.

영희: 엄마, 쟤 깨워 주지 마! 쟤 백 번 깨워도 못 일어나. 야, 김철수! 너 알람 맞춰 놓고 자! 엄마 귀찮게 하지 말고.

철수: 아, 아니야! 이번엔 진짜 일어날 수 있어. 엄마 꼭 깨워 주세요.

엄마: 알았어, 알았어.

영희: 아, 엄마! 그냥 알람 맞추라고 해!

철수: 아, 누나. 진짜 왜 그래!

엄마: 둘 다 조용히 해! 딱 여섯 시에 깨우면 돼?

철수: 네. 딱 여섯 시요! 그때처럼 또 다섯 시 반인데 여섯 시라고 깨우면 안 돼요!

엄마: 너 깨워도 잘 못 일어나니까 그렇지! 근데 왜 이렇게 일찍 일어나려고? 아침 여섯 시에 일어나서 뭐 하게?

철수: 아, 내일 저 친구들이랑 놀러 가기로 했어요.

엄마: 어디로?

English Translation

Cheol-su: Mom, please wake me up at 6 o'clock tomorrow.

Mother: 6 o'clock? 6 in the morning?

Cheol-su: Yes.

Yeong-hui: Mom, don't wake him up. He can never get up even if you try a hundred times. Hey, Cheol-su! Set your own alarm. Don't bother Mom.

Cheol-su: No, no! This time, I can really get up. Mom, please wake me up.

Mother: Okay, okay.

Yeong-hui: Come on, Mom! Tell him to just set his alarm.

Cheol-su: Hey, what's wrong with you?

Mother: Be quiet, both of you. You need me to wake you up at exactly 6 o'clock?

Cheol-su: Yes. At 6 o'clock sharp. Don't wake me up at 5:30 like last time telling me it's 6 o'clock, okay?

Mother: I did that because you can't get up even if I wake you up. But, why do you want to get up so early? What will you do after getting up at 6 in the morning?

Cheol-su: Oh, I'm going on a trip with my friends tomorrow.

Mother: Where?

철수: 설악산이요.

엄마: 이 추운 날 설악산에 왜 가?

철수: 그냥 등산하러 가요.

엄마: 동네 뒷산도 잘 못 오르면서 설악산이 어디라고 가, 이 추위에!

철수: 아, 아니에요. 할 수 있어요!

엄마: 너... 그 같은 과 아름인가 하는 애가 간다고 해서 가려고 하는 거지?

철수: 아... 아... 아니에요! 그냥 등산하고 싶어서 가는 거예요. 어쨌든 내일 꼭 깨워 주세요!

Cheol-su: To Mt. Seorak.

Mother: Why are you going to Mt. Seorak on this cold day?

Cheol-su: Just to go hiking.

Mother: You can't even hike the mountain in the neighborhood. How can you go Mt. Seorak? In such cold weather!

Cheol-su: No, no. I can do it!

Mother: You want to go because that girl, A-reum from the same department is going, right?

Cheol-su: No, no, no! I am going just because I want to go hiking. Anyway, please make sure you wake me up!

Vocabulary

내일	tomorrow
깨워 주다	to wake someone up
아침	morning
쟤	that person (casual)
백 번	a hundred times
일어나다	to wake up
알람	alarm
맞춰 놓다	to set, to adjust
엄마	mother, mom
귀찮다	to feel bothered, to get tired of
조용히	quietly
딱	just, exactly
깨우다	to wake someone up
친구들	friends
놀러 가다	to go out, to go hang out
춥다	to be cold
날	day
등산하다	to climb
동네	neighborhood, area
뒷산	hill behind one's house
오르다	to climb up
추위	cold
같다	to be the same
과	major, department
어쨌든	anyway

Pattern Practice

Study these three grammar patterns that were used in the dialogue and practice!

Pattern I.

VERB + -지 마 casual

Don't VERB.

Sentence Used in the Dialogue

재 깨워 주지 마!

Don't wake him up.

Sample Sentences

이거 먹지 마.

Don't eat this.

가지 마.

Don't go.

Exercises

1. Don't go outside late at night. (to go outside = 밖에 나가다, late at night = 밤 늦게)

   ……›

2. Don't be late tomorrow. (to be late = 늦다, tomorrow = 내일)

   ……›

Answer Key

1. 밤 늦게 밖에 나가지 마. *2.* 내일 늦지 마.

Applied Patterns

VERB + -(으)면 안 돼

→ 걔 깨워 주면 안 돼.

You shouldn't wake him up.

VERB + -지 마세요 formal

→ 걔 깨워 주지 마세요.

Don't wake him up.

Pattern 2.

꼭 VERB + -아/어/여 주세요 formal

Please make sure you VERB. / Be sure to VERB.

Sentence Used in the Dialogue

꼭 깨워 주세요.

Please be sure to wake me up.

Sample Sentences

꼭 와 주세요.

Be sure to come, please.

가기 전에 꼭 창문을 닫아 주세요.
Make sure you close the window before you leave.

Exercises

1. Make sure to call me tomorrow, please. (to call me = 전화하다, tomorrow = 내일)

……›

2. Make sure to turn off the light at night. (to turn off the light = 불을 끄다, at night = 밤에)

……›

Answer Key

1. 내일 꼭 전화해 주세요. *2.* 밤에 꼭 불을 꺼 주세요.

Applied Patterns

꼭 VERB + -아/어/여 주셔야 해요

→ 꼭 깨워 주셔야 해요.
You must wake me up for sure.

꼭 VERB + -아/어/여 줘요

→ 꼭 깨워 줘요.
Be sure to wake me up.

*You sound less formal and slightly more comfortable with the listener if you drop the honorific suffix -시-.

Pattern 3.

VERB + -(으)면 돼? casual

I just have to VERB?

Sentence Used in the Dialogue

여섯 시에 깨우면 돼?

I just have to wake you up at 6 o'clock?

Sample Sentences

지금 전화하면 돼?

I just have to call you now?

이따 거기로 가면 돼?

I just have to go there later?

Exercises

1. I just have to pass this on? (to pass this on = 이것만 전달해 주다)

   ……〉

2. I just have to wait here? (to wait here = 여기서 기다리다)

   ……〉

Answer Key
1. 이것만 전달해 주면 돼? *2.* 여기서 기다리면 돼?

Applied Patterns

VERB + -(으)면 되지?

→ 여섯 시에 깨우면 되지?

I just have to wake you up at 6 o'clock, right?

VERB + -(으)면 되나요? formal

→ 여섯 시에 깨우면 되나요?

I just have to wake you up at 6 o'clock?

어머, 잘 어울리시네요.

Wow, it looks great on you.

Clothing Store

29.900

Dialogue in Korean

점원: 어서 오세요. 찾으시는 스타일 있으세요?

태희: 아, 그냥 둘러볼게요.

점원: 네, 편하게 보세요.

태희: 혜리야, 이거 어때? 요즘 이런 스타일이 유행이라는데?

혜리: 요즘에 진짜 이런 스타일이 대세더라. 근데 난 이런 스타일 안 입어 봐서 안 어울릴 거 같은데?

태희: 한번 입어 봐. 이거 입어 봐도 되죠?

점원: 네, 입어 보세요. 탈의실은 이쪽에 있어요.

혜리: 알았어. 입어 볼게. 넌 다른 옷 보고 있어.

태희: 응. 알았어.

점원: 어머, 잘 어울리시네요. 오늘 이 옷만 계속 팔렸어요. 이게 지금 마지막 남은 옷이에요.

혜리: 진짜요? 아, 근데 뭔가 이상한데?

점원: 그래요? 얼굴이 하얘서 빨간색 입으니까 정말 잘 어울리는데.

혜리: 그래요? 어울리는 거 같기도 하고...

English Translation

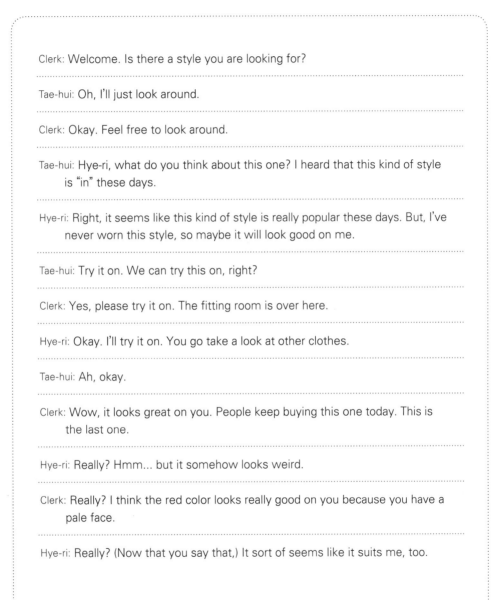

Clerk: Welcome. Is there a style you are looking for?

Tae-hui: Oh, I'll just look around.

Clerk: Okay. Feel free to look around.

Tae-hui: Hye-ri, what do you think about this one? I heard that this kind of style is "in" these days.

Hye-ri: Right, it seems like this kind of style is really popular these days. But, I've never worn this style, so maybe it will look good on me.

Tae-hui: Try it on. We can try this on, right?

Clerk: Yes, please try it on. The fitting room is over here.

Hye-ri: Okay. I'll try it on. You go take a look at other clothes.

Tae-hui: Ah, okay.

Clerk: Wow, it looks great on you. People keep buying this one today. This is the last one.

Hye-ri: Really? Hmm... but it somehow looks weird.

Clerk: Really? I think the red color looks really good on you because you have a pale face.

Hye-ri: Really? (Now that you say that,) It sort of seems like it suits me, too.

점원: 가격도 얼마나 저렴하게 나왔는데요. 완전 거저예요. 이 옷은 없어서 못 팔아요.

혜리: 진짜 별로 안 비싸긴 하네요.

점원: 아휴, 오늘 이 옷만 계속 팔렸다니까요. 있을 때 사 가요.

혜리: 잠깐만요. 태희야! 태희야, 이리 와 봐. 어때? 괜찮아? 잘 어울리는 거 같아?

태희: 아... 음... 근데 좀 작은 거 아냐?

점원: 아니에요. 요즘 타이트하게 입어야지, 누가 크게 입어요.

혜리: 그래? 작은 거 같아? 좀 이상한 거 같긴 해.

태희: 음... 색깔도 너무 튀는 거 같아. 얼마야? 비싸네!

혜리: 그래? 맞아, 비싼 거 같기도 해.

태희: 빨리 갈아입어. 다른 데 가 보자.

점원: 이 옷 없어서 못 파는 건데. 나중에 후회하지 말아요.

혜리: 아, 그래요? 고민되네, 어쩌지?

태희: 저희 다른 곳 한 번만 보고 올게요. 다른 데도 보고 오자. 옷은 바로 사면 후회해.

혜리: 알았어. 옷 갈아입고 나올게.

Clerk: The price is so cheap as well. It's almost free. This one is selling very quickly.

Hye-ri: True, it's not very expensive.

Clerk: Yeah, I told you that people keep buying this. Buy it while we have it in stock.

Hye-ri: Wait a moment. Tae-hui, Tae-hui, come over here. How is it? Is it okay? Do you think it looks good on me?

Tae-hui: Ah... well... but isn't it a bit small for you?

Clerk: No. You should wear tight clothes these days. Who wears big sizes?

Hye-ri: Really? You think it's small? It does look a bit weird.

Tae-hui: Um... I think the colors are too loud, too. How much is it? It's expensive!

Hye-ri: Yeah? You're right. Maybe it's too expensive.

Tae-hui: Hurry up and go change. Let's go check out another place.

Clerk: These clothes are really popular and never in stock. Don't regret it later.

Hye-ri: Oh, really? It's hard to decide. What should I do?

Tae-hui: We're going to look at one other place and come back. Let's go look at another place. If you buy clothes right away (without thinking it through), then you will regret it.

Hye-ri: Okay. I will go change and come (back) out.

Vocabulary

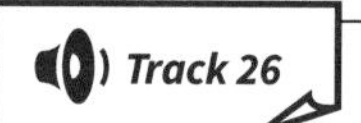

찾다	to look for
둘러보다	to look around
편하게	freely, comfortably, conveniently
보다	to see, to watch
요즘	these days
유행	fashion, trend
대세	general trend, general tendency
입어 보다	to try on (clothes or other fashion items)
어울리다	to suit, to look good on
탈의실	fitting room
다른	different
옷	clothes
계속	continuously, consecutively
팔리다	to be sold
남다	to remain, to be left
이상하다	to be strange, to be weird
얼굴	face
하얗다	to be white, to be fair, to be pale skinned
빨간색	red color
입다	to put on, to wear
가격	price
저렴하다	to be cheap, to be reasonable, to be inexpensive
거저	for free
별로	not really, not particularly
작다	to be small
색깔	color
튀다	to stand out, to be showy
갈아입다	to change (clothes)
후회하다	to regret
고민	worry

Pattern Practice

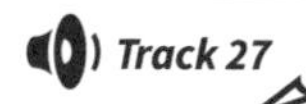

Study these three grammar patterns that were used in the dialogue and practice!

Pattern I.

그냥 VERB + -(으)ㄹ게요 formal

I will just VERB.

Sentence Used in the Dialogue

그냥 둘러 볼게요.

I will just look around.

Sample Sentences

그냥 앉아 있을게요.

I will just sit here.

그냥 안 나갈게요.

I will just not go out.

Exercises

1. I will just buy this one. (to buy this one = 이걸로 사다)

……〉

2. I will just come later. (to come later = 다음에 오다)

……〉

Answer Key

1. 그냥 이걸로 살게요. *2.* 그냥 다음에 올게요.

Applied Patterns

그냥 VERB + -(으)려고요

→ 그냥 둘러 보려고요.

I'm just going to look around.

그냥 VERB + -겠습니다

→ 그냥 둘러 보겠습니다.

I'll just look around.

*The suffix -겠- can mean either an assumption or intention, and in this case it means intention. Use -겠습니다 to politely tell the listener what you will do.

Pattern 2.

VERB/ADJECTIVE + -았/었/였다니까요 formal

I told you that (someone/something) PAST TENSE VERB / was/were ADJECTIVE.

Sentence Used in the Dialogue

오늘 이 옷만 계속 팔렸다니까요.

I told you that people keep buying this.

Sample Sentences

걔가 진짜 그렇게 말했다니까요.

I told you that he really said that.

내가 정말 봤다니까요.

I told you that I really saw it.

Exercises

1. I told you that it really tasted good then. (really = 정말, to taste good = 맛있다, then = 그때는)

   ……›

2. I told you that they said it will be raining today. (to be raining = 비 오다, today = 오늘)

   ……›

Answer Key

1. 그때는 정말 맛있었다니까요. *2.* 오늘 비 온다고 했다니까요.

Applied Patterns

VERB/ADJECTIVE + -았/었/였다고 했잖아요

→ 오늘 이 옷만 계속 팔렸다고 했잖아요.

I told you that people keep buying this.

*-다니까요 is short for -다고 하니까요 or -다고 말하니까요. -다니까요 and -다고 했잖아요 basically mean the same thing. Both expressions are used when you want to emphasize that you already said something that the listener seems to be missing or misunderstanding.

VERB/ADJECTIVE + -았/었/였다니까 casual

→ 오늘 이 옷만 계속 팔렸다니까.

I told you that people keep buying this.

Pattern 3.

VERB + -(으)면 VERB + -아/어/여 casual

If you VERB, then you will VERB.

Sentence Used in the Dialogue

옷은 바로 사면 후회해.

If you buy clothes right away (without thinking it through), then you will regret it.

Sample Sentences

옷 이렇게 입으면 감기 걸려.

If you dress like that, then you will catch a cold.

늦게 자면 내일 지각해.

If you go to bed late, then you will be late tomorrow.

Exercises

1. If you sleep now, you won't get to see that. (to sleep now = 지금 자다, to get to see that = 그거 못 보다)

   ……›

2. If you eat all of this, you will have a stomachache. (to eat all of this = 이거 다 먹다, to have a stomachache = 배 아프다)

……〉

Answer Key

1. 지금 자면 그거 못 봐. *2.* 이거 다 먹으면 배 아파.

Applied Patterns

VERB + -(으)면 VERB + -(으)ㄹ 수도 있어

→ 옷은 바로 사면 후회할 수도 있어.

If you buy clothes right away (without thinking it through), you might regret it.

*Instead of saying 후회해, which means "you will regret it", by saying 후회할 수도 있어, you mean that the listener "might regret it".

VERB + -(으)면 VERB + -(으)ㄹ 지도 몰라

→ 옷은 바로 사면 후회할 지도 몰라.

If you buy clothes right away (without thinking it through), you might regret it.

*Both -(으)ㄹ 수도 있어 and -(으)ㄹ 지도 몰라 mean "you might". However, -(으)ㄹ 수도 있어 more commonly focuses on the possibility of something positive, while -(으)ㄹ 지도 몰라 more frequently focuses on the possibility of something negative happening.

이 신발 어때?

What do you think of these shoes?

Shoe Store

Dialogue in Korean

미선: 오빠, 백화점까지 왔는데 옷이나 신발 사고 싶은 거 없어?

정배: 좀 있으면 겨울인데 가지고 있는 신발이 다 낡았더라고. 그래서 신발 하나 사고 싶어.

미선: 그래. 그러면 신발 가게에 먼저 가 보자.

정배: 오, 마침 세일하고 있네. 저기 저 브랜드부터 보자.

미선: 응. 가격대는 얼마 정도 생각하고 있어?

정배: 10만원 안팎이면 좋을 것 같아.

미선: 오빠, 이 신발 어때?

정배: 글쎄, 나는 이렇게 화려한 색깔 들어간 건 좀 별로야. 무늬나, 마크가 없는 게 내가 좋아하는 바지랑 잘 어울리거든.

미선: 생각 없이 그냥 사서 신는 줄 알았는데, 아니네?

정배: 아니거든! 이래 봬도 신경 쓰거든! 이거 괜찮다.

미선: 완전 하얗네.

정배: 그렇지. 나는 이런 게 좋더라고.

미선: 때 잘 타겠다.

English Translation

Mi-seon: Oppa. Since we are at a department store, is there anything you want to buy, like clothes or shoes?

Jeong-bae: It's going to be winter soon and I just realized that all the shoes that I have are old. So I want to buy a pair of shoes.

Mi-seon: Okay. Then let's go to the shoe store first.

Jeong-bae: Oh, good timing. They are having a sale. Let's look at that brand over there first.

Mi-seon: Okay. What's the price range you have in mind?

Jeong-bae: I think around 100,000 won will be good.

Mi-seon: How about these shoes?

Jeong-bae: Well, I don't particularly like shoes that have bright colors. I like shoes that have no patterns or logos because they suit the pants that I like to wear.

Mi-seon: I thought you bought and wore just any shoes, but apparently it's not the case, I guess?

Jeong-bae: No, I don't! Contrary to what you think, I do care about my shoes. These look good.

Mi-seon: They are really white.

Jeong-bae: Yeah. I tend to like these kind of shoes.

Mi-seon: They will get dirty easily.

정배: 그게 단점이지.

미선: 그게 뭐야. 그럼 비 오는 날도 못 신고, 눈 오는 날도 못 신는 거야? 그럼 왜 사는 거야?

정배: 하긴... 추울 때 대비하려고 하는데 너무 멋만 신경 쓴 것 같네.

미선: 여기 이 두꺼운 부츠 어때?

정배: 그런 건 보통 여자들이 신고 다니지 않아?

미선: 이건 남성용이야, 오빠. 요새 이런 부츠 신고 다니는 남자들도 많아.

정배: 그렇구나. 한번 신어 봐야지. 사이즈가 270이네. 딱 내 발에 맞겠다.

미선: 오, 진짜 따뜻해 보인다.

정배: 와, 장난 아니야. 신발 안이 엄청나게 따뜻하고 부드러워.

미선: 잘됐다. 가격은 어때?

정배: 4만 원밖에 안 해. 가격도 좋고, 착용감도 좋고. 색깔도 이만하면 좋네.

미선: 그럼 오빠 다른 매장도 가서 더 싼 신발 있는지 봐 보자.

정배: 아니야. 난 이 녀석으로 결정했어.

Jeong-bae: Yeah, that's a drawback.

Mi-seon: Why buy them? If you can't wear them when it rains, and you can't wear them when it snows, then why would you buy them?

Jeong-bae: You have a point. I wanted to get shoes for when it's cold, but I was only thinking about how they look.

Mi-seon: How about these thick boots here?

Jeong-bae: Don't women usually wear those?

Mi-seon: These are for men. There are a lot of men who wear these kinds of boots these days.

Jeong-bae: I see. I will try them on. They are size 270. I think they will perfectly fit my feet.

Mi-seon: Oh, they look really warm.

Jeong-bae: Wow, it's amazing. They are really warm and soft inside.

Mi-seon: That's good. What's the price like?

Jeong-bae: It's only 40,000 won. The price is good, it feels good, and the color is also quite nice.

Mi-seon: Then let's go to another store and see if they have cheaper shoes.

Jeong-bae: No, I've decided on these.

Vocabulary

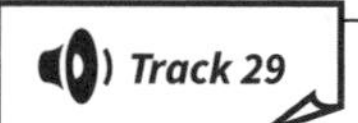

백화점	department store
신발	shoes
낡다	to be old, to be worn out
마침	just in time
가격대	price range
안팎	approximately
화려하다	to be fancy, to be splendid
별로	not really, not particularly
무늬	pattern
바지	pants, trousers
잘 어울리다	to suit, to look good on
신다	to wear (shoes)
신경 쓰다	to care about, to worry about
하얗다	to be white, to be fair
때가 잘 타다	to be stained easily
단점	weak point
눈	snow
대비하다	to prepare for
멋	style
두껍다	to be thick
부츠	boots
남성용	for men
요새	these days
딱 맞다	to fit perfectly
-아/어/여 보이다	to look, to try
엄청나게	tremendously, very
부드럽다	to be soft
착용감	how a piece of clothing feels when worn
싸다	to be cheap
결정하다	to decide

Track 30

Pattern Practice

Study these three grammar patterns that were used in the dialogue and practice!

Pattern 1.

VERB + -고 싶어 casual

I want to VERB.

Sentence Used in the Dialogue

신발 하나 사고 싶어.

I want to buy a pair of shoes.

Sample Sentences

이거 먹고 싶어.

I want to eat this.

집에 가고 싶어.

I want to go home.

Exercises

1. I want to sell my car. (to sell = 팔다, my car = 내 차)

   ......〉

2. I want to go to Korea. (to go to Korea = 한국에 가다)

   ......〉

Answer Key

1. 내 차 팔고 싶어. *2.* 한국에 가고 싶어.

Applied Patterns

VERB + -았/었/였으면 좋겠어

→ 신발 하나 샀으면 좋겠어.

I hope to buy a pair of shoes.

VERB + -고 싶어요 formal

→ 신발 하나 사고 싶어요

I want to buy a pair of shoes.

Pattern 2.

VERB/ADJECTIVE + -면 좋을 것 같아 casual

It will be good if (someone/something) VERB/ADJECTIVE.

Sentence Used in the Dialogue

10만원 안팎이면 좋을 것 같아.

I think around 100,000 won will be good.

Sample Sentences

빨간색이면 좋을 것 같아.

It will be good if it's red.

너무 안 더우면 좋을 것 같아.

It will be good if it's not too hot.

Exercises

1. It will be good if you come early. (you = 너, to come early = 일찍 오다)

   ......〉

2. It will be good if it's summer. (summer = 여름)

   ......〉

Answer Key

1. 너가 일찍 오면 좋을 것 같아. *2.* 여름이면 좋을 것 같아.

Applied Patterns

-면 좋겠어

→ 10만원 안팎이면 좋겠어.

I think around 100,000 won will be good.

*좋을 것 같아 means "I think it will be good" and the -겠- part in 좋겠어 means that you "assume" that it will be good. The meanings are similar, but you can usually express a stronger opinion with 좋겠어.

-면 좋을 것 같아요 formal

→ 10만원 안팎이면 좋을 것 같아요.

I think around 100,000 won will be good.

Pattern 3.

진짜 ADJECTIVE + -아/어/여 보인다 casual

It looks really ADJECTIVE.

Sentence Used in the Dialogue

진짜 따뜻해 보인다.

It looks really warm.

Sample Sentences

진짜 시원해 보인다.

It looks really cool.

진짜 맛있어 보인다.

It looks really tasty.

Exercises

1. It looks really fun. (to be fun = 재미있다)

 ······〉

2. It looks really tough. (to be tough = 힘들다)

 ······〉

Answer Key

1. 진짜 재미있어 보인다. *2*. 진짜 힘들어 보인다.

Applied Patterns

진짜 ADJECTIVE + -아/어/여 보여

→ 진짜 따뜻해 보여.

It looks really warm.

*보인다 is more of an exclamation, while 보여 is just the plain present tense form.

진짜 ADJECTIVE + -겠다

→ 진짜 따뜻하겠다.

It looks really warm.

*The -겠- suffix signifies assumption, so you are assuming that the item is warm.

그냥 둘러보고 있어요.

We are just browsing.

•

Furniture Store

Dialogue in Korean

점원: 어서 오세요! 침대 보러 오셨어요?

여자: 네. 신혼집에 놓을 침대 보고 있어요.

점원: 아, 결혼 준비하시는구나. 축하드려요.

여자: 감사합니다.

점원: 특별히 봐 둔 제품이 있으신가요?

남자: 아니요. 그런 건 없고, 그냥 둘러보고 있어요.

점원: 아, 그럼 사이즈는 킹 사이즈로 보시나요?

남자: 네. 킹 사이즈 침대요.

점원: 그럼 이런 제품은 어떠세요? 이게 이번에 새로 나온 신상인데 아주 반응이 좋아요.

여자: 아, 네... 이건 가격이 어떻게 되나요?

점원: 신상품이라 가격은 좀 있어요. 천오백만 원이에요. 그런데 이게 가격 대비 정말 좋은 침대예요.

여자: 천오백만 원이요? 더 저렴한 제품은 없나요?

점원: 아, 당연히 있죠. 그런데 이 제품이 제가 신혼부부들한테 가장 강력 추천하는 제품이에요. 라텍스 소재를 써서 오래 사용해도 탄력성이 꾸준히 좋고, 고탄력이어서 충격이나 소음도 흡수가 잘 되고요.

English Translation

Clerk: Welcome. Are you looking for a bed?

Woman: Yeah, we're looking for a bed that we'll put in our new house after our marriage.

Clerk: Oh, you are preparing for your wedding. Congratulations!

Woman: Thank you.

Clerk: Is there a product in particular that you have in mind?

Man: No, we don't have anything in mind. We are just browsing.

Clerk: Then, are you looking for a king size?

Man: Yes, a king size bed.

Clerk: Then how about this product? This is a brand-new one that just came out, and the response has been great.

Woman: I see. How much is this one?

Clerk: It's a brand-new one, so it's a bit high. It's 15 million won. But compared to the price, it's a really good bed.

Woman: 15 million won? Don't you have any cheaper products?

Clerk: Of course, we do. But this product is what I strongly recommend to newlyweds. It's made of latex, so even after long-time use, the elasticity is consistent, and because it's highly elastic, it absorbs shock and noise very well.

남자: 아, 네. 저기... 저희는...

점원: 침대 잘못 사면 또 얼마 안 가서 바꿔야 되잖아요. 한번 살 때 오래 쓸 수 있는 걸 사는 게 좋아요. 이건 정말 애들 시집, 장가갈 때까지 써도 아무 문제 없는 매트리스예요.

여자: 아... 저기...

점원: 원단도 너무 좋아요. 한번 만져 보세요. 그리고...

남자: 아니, 저기요! 침대 잘 봤고요. 좀 더 둘러볼게요.

점원: 아... 그러실래요? 네, 그럼 둘러보고 다시 오세요!

Man: Oh, um... Well... we...

Clerk: If you buy the wrong bed, you have to change it soon, you know. It's better to buy something that you can use for a long time when you buy your first one. This is a mattress that you can use without any problem until your children get married.

Woman: Oh, um...

Clerk: The fabric is also really good. Touch it. And...

Man: No, wait. Thanks for showing us the beds. We'll look around more.

Clerk: Oh, you will? Okay. Then look around and come again!

Vocabulary

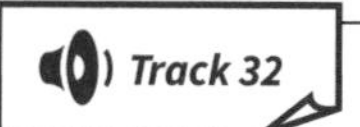

신혼집	newly-married couple's house
놓다	to put
결혼	wedding, marriage
축하하다	to congratulate, to celebrate
특별히	especially, specially, particularly
봐 두다	to take a look at, to look and have in mind
제품	goods, product
둘러보다	to look around
새로 나오다	to have been released recently
신상(품)	new product
반응	response
대비	compared to, comparison
저렴하다	to be cheap, to be reasonable, to be inexpensive
당연히	of course, absolutely
가장	the most
강력히	strongly, firmly
소재	material
오래	long, for a long time
탄력성	elasticity
꾸준히	steadily, consistently, constantly
고탄력	high elasticity
충격	impact, shock
소음	noise
흡수	absorption
바꾸다	to change
시집	getting married (for women)
장가	getting married (for men)
문제	problem
원단	fabric, material
만져 보다	to try touching

Track 33

Pattern Practice

Study these three grammar patterns that were used in the dialogue and practice!

Pattern I.

VERB + -(으)러 오셨어요? formal

Did you come to VERB?

Sentence Used in the Dialogue

침대 보러 오셨어요?

Did you come to look for a bed?

Sample Sentences

휴대폰 고치러 오셨어요?

Did you come to fix your phone?

쇼핑하러 오셨어요?

Did you come to shop?

Exercises

1. Did you come to watch a movie? (to watch a movie = 영화 보다)

   ······〉

2. Did you come to exercise? (to exercise = 운동하다)

   ······〉

Answer Key

1. 영화 보러 오셨어요? *2.* 운동하러 오셨어요?

Applied Patterns

어떤 거 VERB + -(으)러 오셨어요?

→ 어떤 거 보러 오셨어요?

What did you come to look for?

VERB + -(으)려고 오셨어요?

→ 침대 보려고 오셨어요?

Did you come to look for a bed?

Pattern 2.

NOUN + -은/는 없나요? formal

Don't you have NOUN? / Isn't there NOUN?

Sentence Used in the Dialogue

더 저렴한 제품은 없나요?

Don't you have any cheaper products?

Sample Sentences

분홍색은 없나요?

Don't you have a pink one?

더 큰 사이즈는 없나요?

Don't you have a bigger size?

Exercises

1. Don't you have a scary movie? (scary movie = 무서운 영화)

……〉

2. Isn't there anything more that you need? (anything more that you need = 더 필요한 것)

……〉

Answer Key

1. 무서운 영화는 없나요? *2.* 더 필요한 것은 없나요?

Applied Patterns

NOUN + -은/는 없어요?

→ 더 저렴한 제품은 없어요?

Don't you have any cheaper products?

*If you say -없나요?, your question sounds less direct. If you want to sound more direct, you can say 없어요?.

NOUN + -은/는 없어? casual

→ 더 저렴한 제품은 없어?

Don't you have any cheaper products?

Pattern 3.

한번 VERB + -아/어/여 보세요 formal

Try VERB-ing.

Sentence Used in the Dialogue

한번 만져 보세요.

Try touching it.

Sample Sentences

한번 봐 보세요.

Try looking at it.

한번 들어 보세요.

Try listening to it.

Exercises

1. Try reading it. (to read = 읽다)

   ......〉

2. Try calling. (to call = 전화하다)

   ......〉

Answer Key

1. 한번 읽어 보세요 *2*. 한번 전화해 보세요.

Applied Patterns

한번 VERB + -아/어/여 봐요

→ 한번 만져 봐요.

Try touching it.

*-아/어/여 보세요 is a very good way to say "Try + V-ing" in a formal and polite way, but changing 보세요 to 봐요 makes you sound much less formal. Depending on how you say it, you can even sound rude.

한번 VERB + -아/어/여 보실래요?

→ 한번 만져 보실래요?

Do you want to try touching it?

저희 제품 써 보신 적 있으세요?

Have you used our products before?

•

Cosmetics Store

make up
Men's
Bobby umber

Dialogue in Korean

연지: 여기 '겟잇뷰티' 블라인드 테스트에서 1등한 클렌징 오일이 어떤 거예요?

직원: 아, 고객님, 이 제품 말씀하시는 건가요?

연지: 네. 그거 하나 주세요.

직원: 다른 거 더 필요하신 건 없으세요?

연지: 네, 없어요.

직원: 지금 50,000원 이상 구매하시면 여행용 샘플 4종 키트 증정해 드리고 있거든요.

연지: 아... 토너도 다 떨어져서 사야 되긴 하는데...

직원: 토너요? 토너는 이쪽에 있습니다. 저희 제품 써 보신 적 있으세요?

연지: 아니요. 토너는 여기 거 안 써 봤어요. 어떤 게 제일 인기가 많아요?

직원: 이 제품 같은 경우에는 아무래도 가격이 저렴해서 인기가 많구요. 이 제품은 민감성 피부 전용으로 나온 제품이에요. 피부가 민감한 편이세요?

연지: 아니요. 근데 피부가 건조해서 좀 촉촉한 거 쓰고 싶어요.

직원: 아, 그럼 이 제품 어떠세요? 보습력은 이게 가장 좋아요. 정제수 대신 하라케케 추출물을 넣어서 만든 제품이에요.

연지: 오!

English Translation

Yeon-ji: Which of these is the cleansing oil that took first place in the blind test on "Get It Beauty"?

Clerk: Oh, do you mean this product?

Yeon-ji: Yes. Please give me one of those.

Clerk: Is there anything else that you need?

Yeon-ji: No, there isn't.

Clerk: Right now, if you buy more than 50,000 won's worth of products, we are giving away a 4-product travel kit.

Yeon-ji: Oh, I did run out of skin toner so I need to buy another one.

Clerk: A toner? Toners are over here. Have you used our products before?

Yeon-ji: No, I haven't used a toner from this brand. Which is the most popular?

Clerk: This product is popular mainly because it's inexpensive. As for this product, it's a product that was made exclusively for sensitive skin. Do you have sensitive skin?

Yeon-ji: No, but my skin is a bit dry so I want to use something moisturizing.

Clerk: Then how about these? This one is the best in terms of moisturizing. This product was made using Harakake extract instead of refined water.

Yeon-ji: Oh!

직원: 한번 발라 보시겠어요? 사용감이 가볍고 산뜻하면서도 촉촉해요.

연지: 좋네요. 냄새도 좋고.

직원: 같은 라인 수분크림이랑 세트로 구매하시면 15% 할인 받으실 수 있는데, 이걸로 드릴까요?

연지: 아, 아니요. 그냥 토너만 주세요.

직원: 네. 더 필요한 건 없으시고요?

연지: 네, 없어요.

직원: 이쪽에서 계산 도와 드릴게요. 멤버십 카드 있으세요?

연지: 아니요. 하나 만들게요.

직원: 네. 여기 표시된 곳들만 작성해 주시겠어요?

연지: 네.

직원: 그리고 고객님, 저희 DM 수신 동의해 주시면 정기적으로 할인 쿠폰 받아 보실 수 있는데, 받아 보시겠어요?

연지: 그건 괜찮아요.

직원: 네, 그럼 계산 도와 드리겠습니다. 할부 몇 개월로 해 드릴까요?

연지: 일시불로 해 주세요.

직원: 네. 주차하셨어요?

연지: 아니요.

Clerk: Do you want to try applying it? It feels light and fresh yet moist.

Yeon-ji: It's good. It smells good too.

Clerk: If you buy this as a set with the moisturizing cream from the same product line, you can get a 15% discount. Would you like to get this?

Yeon-ji: Um, no. Just give me the toner.

Clerk: Okay. Anything else you need?

Yeon-ji: No, nothing.

Clerk: Let me help you pay over here. Do you have a membership card?

Yeon-ji: No, I will make one.

Clerk: Okay. Would you fill in these marked sections only?

Yeon-ji: Sure.

Clerk: And also, if you agree to receive our direct mail, you can regularly receive discount coupons. Would you like to receive them?

Yeon-ji: No, thanks.

Clerk: Okay, then you can pay now. Would you like to pay in monthly installments?

Yeon-ji: No installments.

Clerk: Okay. Did you park here?

Yeon-ji: No.

직원: 네. 여기 있습니다. 5만원 이상 구매하셔서 여행용 샘플 4종 키트 넣어 드렸구요. 구매하신 토너랑 같은 라인으로 수분크림 샘플도 챙겨 드렸어요.

연지: 네, 감사합니다. 안녕히 계세요.

Clerk: Okay. Here you go. Since you bought more than 50,000 won's worth of products, I've put in the 4-product travel kit and I've also added some moisturizing cream samples in the same product line as the toner that you bought.

Yeon-ji: Okay, thanks. Bye.

Vocabulary

고객님	customer (honorific)
말씀하다	to say (honorific)
여행용	for traveling
증정하다	to give as a freebie, to give as a free gift
토너	(skin) toner
이쪽	this side, this way
인기가 많다	to be popular
저렴하다	to be cheap, to be reasonable, to be inexpensive
민감성	sensitiveness, sensibility
전용	exclusive use
보습력	moisturizing ability
추출물	extract
넣다	to put something in, to add
바르다	to wear, to apply
사용감	texture, how something feels when you use it
가볍다	to be light
산뜻하다	to be fresh, to be refreshing
촉촉하다	to be moist, to be moisturizing
수분크림	moisturizer, moisture cream
도와 드리다	to help (honorific)
멤버십 카드	membership card
표시	mark
작성하다	to fill out
수신	reception
동의하다	to agree
정기적으로	regularly
받아 보다	to receive
할부	monthly installment plan
일시불	lump sum, one-time payment
챙겨 주다	to look after, to tend to, to take care of

Pattern Practice

Study these three grammar patterns that were used in the dialogue and practice!

Pattern I.

NOUN + -이/가 어떤 거예요? formal

Which one is NOUN?

Sentence Used in the Dialogue

'겟잇뷰티' 블라인드 테스트에서 1등한 클렌징 오일이 어떤 거예요?

Which is the cleansing oil that took first place in the blind test on "Get It Beauty"?

Sample Sentences

요즘 제일 잘 나가는 휴대폰이 어떤 거예요?

Which is the most popular cellphone these days?

저 사람이 입고 있는 옷이 어떤 거예요?

Which item is that person wearing?

Exercises

1. Which is the smallest size? (the smallest size = 제일 작은 사이즈)

   ......〉

2. Which is the cheapest product? (the cheapest product = 가장 싼 제품)

   ......〉

Answer Key

1. 제일 작은 사이즈가 어떤 거예요? *2.* 가장 싼 제품이 어떤 거예요?

Applied Patterns

NOUN + -이/가 뭐예요?

→ '겟잇뷰티' 블라인드 테스트에서 1등한 클렌징 오일이 뭐예요?

What is the cleansing oil that took first place in the blind test on "Get It Beauty"?

NOUN 어디 있어요?

→ '겟잇뷰티' 블라인드 테스트에서 1등한 클렌징 오일 어디 있어요?

Where is the cleansing oil that took first place in the blind test on "Get It Beauty"?

Pattern 2.

NOUN 말씀하시는 건가요? formal

Are you saying NOUN? / Do you mean NOUN?

Sentence Used in the Dialogue

이 제품 말씀하시는 건가요?

Do you mean this product?

Sample Sentences

이거 말씀하시는 건가요?

Do you mean this one?

어제 봤던 그 식당 말씀하시는 건가요?

Do you mean the restaurant that we saw yesterday?

Exercises

1. Do you mean the white one? (the white one = 하얀색)

 ......>

2. Do you mean that book over there on the shelf? (that book over there on the shelf = 선반 위에 있는 저 책)

 ......>

Answer Key

1. 하얀색 말씀하시는 건가요? *2.* 선반 위에 있는 저 책 말씀하시는 건가요?

Applied Patterns

NOUN 맞나요?

→ 이 제품 맞나요?

Is this product what you want?

NOUN 찾으시는 건가요?

→ 이 제품 찾으시는 건가요?

Are you looking for this product?

Pattern 3.

VERB/ADJECTIVE + -(느)ㄴ 편이세요? formal

Do you tend to VERB? / Are you more ADJECTIVE type?

Sentence Used in the Dialogue

피부가 민감한 편이세요?

Do you have sensitive skin?

Sample Sentences

내성적인 편이세요?

Are you more of an introspective type of person?

매운 걸 잘 먹는 편이세요?

Do you tend to be good at eating spicy food?

Exercises

1. Do you tend to eat a lot? (to eat = 먹다, a lot = 많이)

   ......〉

2. Do you tend to sleep more in the morning? (to sleep more in the morning = 아침잠이 많다)

   ......〉

Answer Key
1. 많이 먹는 편이세요? *2*. 아침 잠이 많은 편이세요?

Applied Patterns

VERB/ADJECTIVE + -(느)ㄴ 편이에요?

→ 피부가 민감한 편이에요?
Do you have sensitive skin?

*By removing the suffix -시-, you sound a little less formal.

VERB/ADJECTIVE + -(느)ㄴ 쪽에 속하세요?

→ 피부가 민감한 쪽에 속하세요?
Are you more of a sensitive skin type?

혹시 몰라서 핫팩 가져왔어요.

I brought some heat packs just in case.

•

Blind Date

②
홍대
9번출구

Dialogue in Korean

인서: 안녕하세요. 오늘 만나기로 한 기주 씨 맞죠?

기주: 안녕하세요. 인서 씨 되시죠?

인서: 네. 맞아요. 오늘 많이 춥죠?

기주: 네. 갑자기 많이 추워졌네요.

인서: 혹시 몰라서 핫팩 가져왔는데, 이거 쓰세요.

기주: 정말요? 인서 씨는요?

인서: 저는 주머니에 몇 개 더 있어요.

기주: 고마워요.

인서: 식사 아직 안 하셨죠?

기주: 네.

인서: 제가 몇 군데 괜찮은 곳 찾아봤는데요, 파스타 잘하는 곳이 있더라고요.

기주: 파스타도 좋긴 한데, 오늘은 좀 다른 거 먹었으면 해요. 보쌈 어때요?

인서: 네? 보쌈이요? 보통은 소개팅하면서 보쌈 같은 거 잘 안 먹지 않나요?

English Translation

In-seo: Hi. You are Gi-ju, right? We are supposed to meet today.

Gi-ju: Hi. You must be In-seo, right?

In-seo: Yes, that's right. It's really cold today, right?

Gi-ju: Yeah, it has become very cold all of a sudden.

In-seo: I brought some heat packs just in case. You can use this.

Gi-ju: Really? How about you?

In-seo: I have a few more in my pocket.

Gi-ju: Thank you.

In-seo: You haven't eaten yet, right?

Gi-ju: Right.

In-seo: I've looked up some nice places, and there is a good pasta place near here.

Gi-ju: Pasta sounds good, but why don't we have something different today? How about bossam (boiled pork)?

In-seo: Huh? Bossam? People don't normally eat bossam on a blind date, do they?

기주: 뭐, 어때요? 따뜻한 보쌈 먹으면서 소주도 한 잔씩 하면 더 편해질 것 같지 않아요?

인서: 사실 저도 오늘 같은 날씨에 파스타는 별로라고 생각했었어요.

기주: 제가 아는 보쌈집 있으니까 그리로 가요.

인서: 네. 좋아요.

기주: 석진이하고는 어떻게 아는 사이예요?

인서: 석진이가 군대 있을 때 제 후임이었어요. 군대에 있을 때 친하게 지내서 제대한 후에도 계속 연락하고 지냈어요. 기주 씨는요?

기주: 석진이하고 저하고 대학 동창이에요. 졸업하고 친구들이랑 같이 저녁 먹을 자리가 있었는데, 제가 혼자라고 하니까 소개팅을 주선하더라고요.

인서: 그렇군요. 근데, 기주 씨 같은 분이 지금 혼자라고 하니까 이해가 잘 안 돼요.

기주: 왜요?

인서: 이렇게 예쁘시잖아요. 주위에서 대시하는 사람들 많았을 것 같아요.

기주: 하하하. 아니에요.

Gi-ju: Well, what's wrong with that? Some warm bossam and some soju will break the ice, don't you think?

In-seo: Actually, I was also thinking that pasta doesn't suit today's weather.

Gi-ju: There is a bossam place that I know, so let's go there.

In-seo: Okay. Sounds good.

Gi-ju: How do you know Seokjin (who arranged this blind date)?

In-seo: Seokjin was a junior soldier when I was in the army. We got along well, so even after we finished our service, we kept in touch. How about you?

Gi-ju: Seokjin and I are university friends. We had dinner with some friends after graduation, and when I said that I was single, he arranged this blind date.

In-seo: I see. But I don't quite understand how someone like you is single now.

Gi-ju: Why?

In-seo: You're so pretty. There must have been a lot of people around you who hit on you.

Gi-ju: Hahaha. Not really.

Vocabulary

갑자기	suddenly	친하다	to be close
가져오다	to bring	제대하다	to be released from one's military duty, to finish one's military service
주머니	pocket	계속	continuously, consecutively
식사	meal	연락하다	to contact
군데	place, spot	대학	college
곳	place	동창	alumnus, alumna
다른	different	졸업하다	to graduate
소개팅	blind date	저녁	dinner
소주	soju (Korean distilled spirit)	자리	occasion
잔	numerical counter for cups or glasses	혼자	alone, by oneself
편하다	to be comfortable	주선하다	to arrange, to organize (meeting)
날씨	weather	분	numerical counter for people (honorific)
사이	relationship, relations	이해	understanding
군대	military	주위	surroundings, around oneself
후임	successor, junior	대시하다	to hit on someone

Pattern Practice

Track 39

Study these three grammar patterns that were used in the dialogue and practice!

Pattern I.

ADJECTIVE + -아/어/여졌네요 formal

I see that (someone/something) has become/became ADJECTIVE.

Sentence Used in the Dialogue

많이 추워졌네요.

I see that it has become very cold.

Sample Sentences

두 사람 친해졌네요.

I see that you two have become close.

뜨거워졌네요.

I see that it has become hot.

Exercises

1. I see that it became more fun. (to be more fun = 더 재미있다)

   ......〉

2. I see that it became more expensive than yesterday. (to be more expensive than yesterday = 어제보다 비싸다)

   ......〉

Answer Key

1. 더 재미있어졌네요. *2.* 어제보다 비싸졌네요.

Applied Patterns

ADJECTIVE + -아/어/여졌어요

→ 많이 추워졌어요.

It has become very cold.

ADJECTIVE + -아/어/여졌네 casual

→ 많이 추워졌네.

I see that it has become very cold.

Pattern 2.

VERB + -았/었/였으면 해요 formal

Why don't we VERB?

Sentence Used in the Dialogue

오늘은 좀 다른 거 먹었으면 해요.

Why don't we have something different today?

Sample Sentences

다른 영화를 봤으면 해요.

Why don't we watch another movie?

잠깐 만났으면 해요.
Why don't we meet for a second?

Exercises

1. Why don't we go out a little early? (to go out = 나가다, a little early = 조금 일찍)

   ……›

2. Why don't we change the place where we will meet? (to change = 바꾸다, the place where we will meet = 만날 장소)

   ……›

Answer Key
1. 조금 일찍 나갔으면 해요. *2.* 만날 장소를 바꿨으면 해요.

Applied Patterns

VERB + -고 싶어요

→ 오늘은 좀 다른 거 먹고 싶어요.
I want to eat something different today.

VERB + -(으)면 어떨까요?

→ 오늘은 좀 다른 거 먹으면 어떨까요?
How about we have something different today?

*어떨까요? literally means "How will it be?" or "How do you think it will be?"

Pattern 3.

Someone/Something + -은/는/이/가 NOUN + -(이)라고 생각했었어요 formal

I was thinking that someone/something was NOUN / I used to think that someone/something was NOUN

Sentence Used in the Dialogue

파스타는 별로라고 생각했었어요.

I was thinking that pasta was not a good choice.

*별로 is not a noun grammatically, but in everyday conversations, it's often used as a noun meaning "something that is not so good."

Sample Sentences

이 두 개가 같은 거라고 생각했었어요.

I used to think that these two were the same thing.

경화 씨가 학생이라고 생각했었어요.

I was thinking that Kyung-hwa was a student.

Exercises

1. I used to think that Hyunwoo was the only son. (Hyunwoo = 현우 씨, only son = 외아들)

   ……›

2. I used to think that that was the best way. (that = 그게, the best way = 최선의 방법)

……›

Answer Key

1. 현우 씨가 외아들이라고 생각했었어요. *2.* 그게 최선의 방법이라고 생각했었어요.

Applied Patterns

Someone/Something + -은/는/이/가 NOUN + -(이)라고 생각했어요

→ 파스타는 별로라고 생각했어요.

I was also thinking that pasta doesn't suit today's weather.

*You can drop the additional suffix -었- because 했어요 is enough to indicate that the action was done in the past.

Someone/Something + -은/는/이/가 NOUN + -(이)라고 생각했었어 casual

→ 파스타는 별로라고 생각했었어.

I was also thinking that pasta doesn't suit today's weather.

영화 시간 얼마 안 남았으니까 들어갈까요?

Since there is not a lot of time before the movie starts, shall we go inside?

•

Movie Date

월터와 핑크맨

Dialogue in Korean

정석: 민아 씨, 여기요.

민아: 오래 기다리셨어요? 죄송해요.

정석: 아니에요. 괜찮아요.

민아: 우리 오늘 뭐 할까요?

정석: 민아 씨, 영화 좋아하세요?

민아: 영화 좋아해요. 우리 그럼 영화 볼까요? 근데 주말이라서 미리 예매 안 해 놓으면 표가 없을 거 같은데요.

정석: 아, 혹시 몰라서 민아 씨 기다리면서 제가 표가 있나 핸드폰으로 확인했는데 아직 자리가 있더라고요.

민아: 아, 그래요? 그럼 어차피 조금만 내려가면 영화관이니까 거기로 갈까요?

정석: 네, 좋아요. 민아 씨는 어떤 영화 좋아해요?

민아: 음, 전 영화는 다 좋아해요.

정석: 최근에 본 영화는 뭐예요?

민아: 최근에 본 영화요? 최근에는 영화를 못 봤어요. 마지막으로 본 영화가 어바웃 타임이에요.

정석: 진짜요? 저도 어바웃 타임 봤어요.

English Translation

Jeong-seok: Min-a, over here.

Min-a: Have you been waiting long? I'm sorry.

Jeong-seok: No, it's alright.

Min-a: What shall we do today?

Jeong-seok: Min-a, do you like movies?

Min-a: I like movies. Then shall we watch a movie? But since it's the weekend, if you don't book in advance, I don't think there will be tickets.

Jeong-seok: Oh, while waiting for you, I checked on my phone to see if there were tickets left, and there are still seats.

Min-a: Oh, really? Then since the movie theater is just down the street, shall we go over there?

Jeong-seok: Yes. Sounds good. What kind of movie do you like?

Min-a: Um, I like all kinds of movies.

Jeong-seok: What is something that you watched recently?

Min-a: A movie that I watched recently? I haven't watched any movies recently. The movie that I saw last was About Time.

Jeong-seok: Really? I saw About Time too.

민아: 정말 감동적이죠? 전 그 영화 세 번 봤어요.

정석: 진짜요? 저도 정말 재미있게 보긴 했어요. 근데 전 같은 영화를 세 번이나 보진 못하겠더라고요.

민아: 그래요? 전 감동적인 영화는 여러 번 보는 편이에요.

정석: 아, 그거 알아요? 최근에 어바웃 타임이랑 비슷한 종류의 영화를 개봉했다고 하더라고요.

민아: 아, 저도 그거 보고 싶었어요. 그 영화 볼까요?

정석: 자리가 있나 한번 볼까요?

민아: 아, 있네요. 저 영화 봐요, 우리.

정석: 좋아요. 잠시만요. 이 영화 3시 타임이요. 성인 2명이고, 자리는 뒷자리로 해 주세요.

민아: 팝콘이랑 콜라도 살까요?

정석: 네, 좋아요. 영화관에서는 꼭 팝콘을 먹어야죠!

민아: 저랑 취향이 좀 비슷하신 거 같아요.

정석: 하하. 진짜 그런 거 같아요. 영화 시간 얼마 안 남았으니까 들어갈까요?

민아: 네, 좋아요.

Min-a: It was really touching, wasn't it? I watched that movie three times.

Jeong-seok: Really? I really enjoyed it too. But I can't watch the same movie three times.

Min-a: Really? I like to watch touching movies several times.

Jeong-seok: Oh, you know what? Recently, I heard that a similar kind of movie to About Time was released.

Min-a: Oh, I've been wanting to watch that movie too. Shall we watch that one?

Jeong-seok: Let's see if there are seats.

Min-a: Oh, there are. Let's watch that movie.

Jeong-seok: Good. Just a second. 2 adults for this movie at 3 o'clock. Please give us seats in the back.

Min-a: Should we buy popcorn and cola too?

Jeong-seok: Yes, sounds good. You gotta have popcorn when you are in a movie theater!

Min-a: I think you and I have similar tastes.

Jeong-seok: Haha. I think we really do. Since there is not a lot of time before the movie starts, shall we go inside?

Min-a: Yes. Sounds good.

Vocabulary

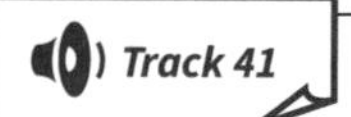

오래	long, for a long time
기다리다	to wait
죄송하다	to be sorry
영화	movie
주말	weekend
미리	in advance
예매	reservation, buying in advance
혹시 모르다	to prepare just in case, to think of the unlikely possibility
확인하다	to check, to confirm
자리	place, spot, seat
내려가다	to go down
영화관	movie theater
최근에	recently
마지막	last
어차피	anyway, after all
감동적이다	to be touching, to be moving
여러 번	several times
비슷하다	to be similar
종류	kind, type
개봉하다	to release (a movie)
보고 싶다	to want to watch
성인	adult
뒷자리	back seat, seat in the back
취향	taste, preference
시간	time
남다	to remain, to be left
들어가다	to go in

Pattern Practice

Study these three grammar patterns that were used in the dialogue and practice!

VERB + -(으)ㄹ까요? formal

Shall we VERB?

Sentence Used in the Dialogue

우리 그럼 영화 볼까요?

Then shall we watch a movie?

Sample Sentences

이거 먹으러 갈까요?

Shall we go eat this?

다음 달에 여행 갈까요?

Shall we travel next month?

Exercises

1. Shall we go now? (to go = 가다, now = 지금)

   ······〉

2. Shall we walk for a bit? (to walk for a bit = 좀 걷다)

   ······〉

Answer Key

1. 지금 갈까요? *2.* 좀 걸을까요?

Applied Patterns

VERB + -(으)ㄹ래요?

→ 우리 그럼 영화 볼래요?

Then do you want to watch a movie?

VERB + -(으)ㄹ까? casual

→ 우리 그럼 영화 볼까?

Then shall we watch a movie?

Pattern 2.

어떤 NOUN 좋아해요? formal

What kind of NOUN do you like?

Sentence Used in the Dialogue

어떤 영화 좋아해요?

What kind of movie do you like?

Sample Sentences

어떤 음악 좋아해요?

What kind of music do you like?

어떤 책 좋아해요?
What kind of book do you like?

Exercises

1. What kind of coffee do you like? (coffee = 커피)

······›

2. What kind of sports do you like? (sports = 스포츠)

······›

Answer Key
1. 어떤 커피 좋아해요? *2.* 어떤 스포츠 좋아해요?

Applied Patterns

무슨 NOUN 좋아해요?

→ 무슨 영화 좋아해요?
What movie do you like?

NOUN 어떤 거 좋아해요?

→ 영화 어떤 거 좋아해요?
Which kind of movie do you like?

*어떤 거 means "what/which kind of thing" or "which one" and it is used after the noun.

Pattern 3.

(Someone/Something) + (-이/가) VERB + -았/었/였다고 하더라고요 formal

They say someone/something PAST TENSE VERB. / I heard that someone/something PAST TENSE VERB.

Sentence Used in the Dialogue

최근에 비슷한 종류의 영화를 개봉했다고 하더라고요.

I heard that a similar kind of movie was recently released.

Sample Sentences

맞은 편에 디저트 가게 오픈했다고 하더라고요.

I heard that a dessert shop opened across the street.

그 애가 대회에서 1등 했다고 하더라고요.

I heard that the kid won first place in the competition.

Exercises

1. I heard that the woman moved last month. (the woman = 그 여자, to move = 이사가다, last month = 지난 달에)

   ……〉

2. I heard that the guy got married. (the guy = 그 남자, to get married = 결혼하다)

······〉

Answer Key

1. 그 여자 지난 달에 이사갔다고 하더라고요. *2.* 그 남자 결혼했다고 하더라고요.

Applied Patterns

(Someone/Something) + (-이/가) VERB + -(느)ㄴ다고 하더라고요

→ 곧 비슷한 종류의 영화를 개봉한다고 하더라고요.

I heard that a similar kind of movie will be released soon.

(Someone/Something) + (-이/가) VERB + -았/었/였다고 들었어요

→ 최근에 비슷한 종류의 영화를 개봉했다고 들었어요.

I heard that a similar kind of movie was recently released.

자전거 오랜만에 타니까 진짜 재밌다!

It was so much fun riding a bike after such a long time.

•

Park

Dialogue in Korean

민수: 자기야, 우리 밥 먹고 뭐 할까?

지연: 음... 글쎄. 오늘 날씨도 좋으니까 야외에서 데이트할까?

민수: 그럴까? 그럼 우리 오늘 한강 공원 갈까?

지연: 오, 그래! 좋아! 그럼 가서 치맥도 먹자!

민수: 그래, 그러자!

민수: 우와, 사람 되게 많다!

지연: 진짜네. 날씨가 좋아서 사람들이 다 밖으로 나왔나 봐.

민수: 응, 그런가 보다. 자기야, 다리 안 아파?

지연: 응, 괜찮아. 날씨가 좋으니까 많이 걸어도 다리가 안 아프네.

민수: 하하. 매일 날씨가 이렇게 좋았으면 좋겠다.

지연: 그러게. 자기야, 여기 자전거 빌려주나 봐. 우리 자전거 탈까?

민수: 그래! 2인용 자전거 빌릴까?

지연: 아니. 따로 탈래. 각자 하나씩 빌리자.

민수: 아니, 그래도 커플들은 원래...

English Translation

Min-su: Sweetheart, what shall we do after eating?

Ji-yeon: Hmm... well. Since the weather is nice, how about a date outside?

Min-su: Shall we? Then shall we go to the Han River park?

Ji-yeon: Oh, yes! Sounds good! Then let's go and have chicken and beer!

Min-su: Yes, let's do that!

Min-su: Wow, there are so many people.

Ji-yeon: There really are. I guess they all came outside since the weather is nice.

Min-su: Yeah, I guess so. Honey, aren't your legs tired?

Ji-yeon: Oh, I'm okay. Since the weather is so nice, my legs don't hurt even if I walk a lot.

Min-su: Haha. I wish the weather was this nice every day.

Ji-yeon: Me, too. Honey, I guess they rent bikes here. Do you want to ride a bike?

Min-su: Yes! Shall we rent a two-person bike?

Ji-yeon: No, I want to ride separately. Let's rent one each.

Min-su: I mean, couples usually...

지연: 아저씨, 1인용 자전거 두 개요!

민수: 우와! 자전거 오랜만에 타니까 진짜 재밌다!

지연: 맞아. 너무 재밌었어. 자기야 나 배고파.

민수: 그치? 나도 이제 슬슬 배고프네. 치맥 시킬까?

지연: 좋지! 반반?

민수: 응, 그러자! 그럼 내가 시킬게! (전화 통화) 아저씨, 여기 한강 공원 마포지구인데요, 양념 반 후라이드 반으로 갖다 주세요.

지연: 맥주도!

민수: 아, 저기 아저씨, 맥주도 가져다... 아... 끊겼네...

지연: 아, 뭐야. 그럼 자기가 맥주 사 와!

민수: 알겠어. 저기 앞에 편의점에서 금방 사 올게!

Ji-yeon: Excuse me, two one-person bikes, please.

Min-su: Wow! It was so much fun riding a bike after such a long time.

Ji-yeon: Yes, it was so much fun. Honey, I'm hungry.

Min-su: Right? I'm getting hungry too. Shall we order chicken and beer?

Ji-yeon: Good! Half and half?

Min-su: Yeah, let's do that. Then let me order it. (On the phone) We are in the Mapo area of the Han River park. We'd like one order of fried chicken, half with seasoning and half without.

Ji-yeon: Beer, too!

Min-su: Oh, also, please bring us beer... Oh, he hung up.

Ji-yeon: Hey! Then you should go buy some beer.

Min-su: Okay. I'll quickly go to the convenience store over there and buy it.

Vocabulary

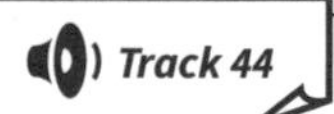

밥	meal
야외	outside
공원	park
치맥	chicken and beer (short term for 치킨과 맥주)
되게	very, so
밖	outside
나오다	to come out
다리	leg
아프다	to hurt, to ache, to be painful
괜찮다	to be okay, to be alright
자전거	bicycle
빌려주다	to lend
타다	to ride
2인용	two-seater
따로	separately, individually, particularly
각자	respectively
빌리다	to borrow
원래	original, existing
오랜만에	in a long time, after not doing so for a long time
배고프다	to be hungry
시키다	to order
반	half
양념	seasoning, spice
갖다 주다	to bring
맥주	beer
끊기다	to lose contact
사다	to buy
편의점	convenient store
금방	soon

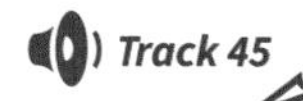

Pattern Practice

Study these three grammar patterns that were used in the dialogue and practice!

Pattern I.

VERB + -고 뭐 할까? casual

What shall we do after VERB-ing?

Sentence Used in the Dialogue

우리 밥 먹고 뭐 할까?

What shall we do after eating?

Sample Sentences

이거 끝내고 뭐 할까?
What shall we do after finishing this?

시험 보고 뭐 할까?
What shall we do after taking the test?

Exercises

1. What shall we do after drinking this? (to drink this = 이거 마시다)

   ······›

2. What shall we do after getting off of work? (to get off of work = 퇴근하다)

   ······›

Answer Key

1. 이거 마시고 뭐 할까? 2. 퇴근하고 뭐 할까?

Applied Patterns

VERB + -고 뭐 하고 싶어?

→ 우리 밥 먹고 뭐 하고 싶어?

What do you want to do after we eat?

VERB + -고 뭐 할까요? formal

→ 우리 밥 먹고 뭐 할까요?

What shall we do after we eat?

Pattern 2.

Someone + -이/가 VERB/ADJECTIVE + -았/었/였나 봐 casual

I guess someone PAST TENSE VERB / was/were ADJECTIVE

Sentence Used in the Dialogue

날씨가 좋아서 사람들이 다 밖으로 나왔나 봐.

I guess they all came outside since the weather is nice.

Sample Sentences

더워서 다들 바다로 갔나 봐.

I guess everyone went to the beach since the weather is hot.

강아지가 심심했나 봐.

I guess the dog was bored.

Exercises

1. I guess he liked you. (he = 저 남자, to like = 좋아하다, you = 너)

……〉

2. I guess Su-yeon hasn't come yet. (to come = 오다, yet = 아직)

……〉

Answer Key

1. 저 남자가 너 좋아했나 봐. *2*. 수연이가 아직 안 왔나 봐.

Applied Patterns

Someone + -이/가 VERB/ADJECTIVE + -(으)ㄴ 것 같아

→ 날씨가 좋아서 사람들이 다 밖으로 나온 것 같아.

I think they all came outside since the weather is nice.

*-나 봐 means "I guess" or "I assume" and -(느)ㄴ 것 같아 means "I think" or "it looks like".

Someone + -이/가 VERB/ADJECTIVE + -았/었/였나 봐요 formal

→ 날씨가 좋아서 사람들이 다 밖으로 나왔나 봐요.

I guess they all came outside since the weather is nice.

Pattern 3.

Something + -이/가 VERB/ADJECTIVE + -았/었/였으면 좋겠다 casual

I wish something PAST TENSE VERB / was/were ADJECTIVE

Sentence Used in the Dialogue

매일 날씨가 이렇게 좋았으면 좋겠다.

I wish the weather was this nice every day.

Sample Sentences

여기가 내 집이었으면 좋겠다.

I wish this was my home.

비가 왔으면 좋겠다.

I wish it rained.

Exercises

1. I wish I won the lottery. (to win the lottery = 로또 당첨되다)

......〉

2. I wish I was good at swimming. (to be good at = 잘하다, swimming = 수영)

......〉

Answer Key

1. (내가) 로또 당첨됐으면 좋겠다. *2.* (내가) 수영(을) 잘했으면 좋겠다.

Applied Patterns

Something + -이/가 VERB/ADJECTIVE + -(으)면 좋겠다

→ 매일 날씨가 이렇게 좋으면 좋겠다.

I wish the weather was this nice every day.

*For expressing wishes, you can use either -았/었/였으면 좋겠다 or -(으)면 좋겠다. The probability that both of these expressions convey is mostly the same.

Something + -이/가 VERB/ADJECTIVE + -(으)면 얼마나 좋을까?

→ 매일 날씨가 이렇게 좋으면 얼마나 좋을까?

How good would it be if the weather was this nice every day?

생각도 안 해 보고 그렇게 거절하는 거야?

You haven't even thought about it and you're rejecting me like that?

•

Rejection

Dialogue in Korean

주희: 영화 진짜 재미있었어. 그치?

준서: 응. 재밌더라.

주희: 오늘 밥도 진짜 맛있었고.

준서: 그러게. 날씨도 좋네. 너가 딱 좋아하는 선선한 날씨다.

주희: 그러네? 오늘 기분 진짜 좋다.

준서: 날씨도 좋은데 조금만 더 걸을까?

주희: 응? 그럴까?

준서: 그러자. 좀 걷고 싶다.

주희: 그래. 근데 너 무슨 일 있어?

준서: 아니. 그런 거 없어. 그냥...

주희: 그냥 뭐?

준서: 주희야. 여기 좀 앉아 봐.

주희: 왜 그러는데? 무슨 일이야?

준서: 우리가 알고 지낸 지 얼마나 됐지?

주희: 우리? 글쎄. 한 8년 됐나? 왜?

English Translation

Juhee: The movie was really fun, wasn't it?

Junseo: Yeah, it was fun.

Juhee: And the food we had today was really good, too.

Junseo: Right. The weather is nice, too. It's the cool weather that you like the most.

Juhee: You're right. I feel really good today.

Junseo: The weather is so nice, shall we walk a little more?

Juhee: Hmm? Shall we?

Junseo: Let's. I want to walk a bit.

Juhee: Okay. But, is something wrong?

Junseo: No, nothing like that. It's just...

Juhee: It's just what?

Junseo: Juhee. Sit down here for a second.

Juhee: Why? What's the matter?

Junseo: How long have we known each other?

Juhee: Us? I don't know... Around 8 years? Why?

준서: 우리가 8년을 친구로 지냈는데 사실 난 이제 너랑 친구만 하긴 싫어.

주희: 응?

준서: 나는 이제 친구 말고 너 남자 친구 하고 싶어.

주희: 휴... 준서야. 우리 이렇게 친구로 지낸 지가 벌써 8년이야.

준서: 그러니까 더 이상 친구 하면 안 될 것 같아.

주희: 우리가 어떻게 남자 친구, 여자 친구가 돼. 넌 나한테 이미 너무 남동생인데...

준서: 넌 정말 내가 남자로 전혀 안 느껴져? 이렇게 매일 붙어 다니는데?

주희: 그러니까. 이렇게 매일 붙어 다니니까 더 내 동생 같아.

준서: 생각도 안 해 보고 그렇게 거절하는 거야?

주희: 생각할 필요도 없어.

준서: 왜?

주희: 넌 내 베스트 프렌드이자 내 남동생이야. 누나한테 흑심 품지 말고 좋은 여자 만나라, 내 동생.

Junseo: We've been friends for 8 years, but to be honest, I don't want to be just a friend anymore.

Juhee: Huh?

Junseo: From now on I don't want to be your friend, I want to be your boyfriend.

Juhee: Ah... Junseo. We've been friends for 8 years already.

Junseo: I know, I'm saying I don't think we should be friends anymore.

Juhee: How can we be boyfriend and girlfriend? You're already too much of a younger brother to me.

Junseo: You really don't see me as a man at all? Even though we're together like this every day?

Juhee: Exactly. We're like this together every day, so you're like a little brother.

Junseo: You haven't even thought about it and you're rejecting me like that?

Juhee: I don't need to think about it.

Junseo: Why?

Juhee: You're my best friend and my little brother. Don't go for me. You should meet a good woman, Junseo.

Vocabulary

영화	movie
재미있다	to be fun, to be interesting
밥	meal
맛있다	to be tasty
날씨	weather
딱	just, exactly
선선하다	to be cool, to be refreshing
기분	feeling, mood
걷다	to walk
일	work, occasion
앉다	to sit
알고 지내다	to go back, to have known each other
친구로 지내다	to be friends with
사실	actually
남자 친구	boyfriend
벌써	already
더 이상	not anymore
이미	already
남동생	younger brother
전혀	not at all
매일	every day
붙어 다니다	to hangout together, to stick together
동생	younger sibling
생각	thought
거절하다	to return, to reject
누나	older sister
흑심	black heart, evil intention
흑심을 품다	have indecent desires (for)
여자	girl, woman
만나다	to meet

Pattern Practice

Study these three grammar patterns that were used in the dialogue and practice!

Pattern I.

VERB + -(으)ㄴ 지 얼마나 됐지? casual

How long has/have (SUBJECT) PAST PARTICIPLE VERB?

Sentence Used in the Dialogue

우리가 알고 지낸 지 얼마나 됐지?

How long have we known each other?

Sample Sentences

시작한 지 얼마나 됐지?

How long has it been since it started?

한국어 공부한 지 얼마나 됐지?

How long have you studied Korean?

Exercises

1. How long have you lived here? (to live here = 여기에서 살다)

......〉

2. How long has it been since the shop opened? (the shop = 그 가게, to open = 오픈하다)

......〉

Answer Key

1. 여기에서 산 지 얼마나 됐지? *2.* 그 가게 오픈한 지 얼마나 됐지?

Applied Patterns

VERB + -(으)ㄴ 지 얼마나 됐어?

→ 우리가 알고 지낸 지 얼마나 됐어?

How long have we known each other?

*됐지? sounds like you are checking a fact or something you already think is true, whereas 됐어? sounds like you are plainly asking.

VERB + -(으)ㄴ 지 얼마나 됐죠? formal

→ 우리가 알고 지낸 지 얼마나 됐죠?

How long have we known each other?

Pattern 2.

VERB + -(으)ㄹ 필요도 없어 casual

You don't need to VERB. / There's no need to VERB.

Sentence Used in the Dialogue

생각할 필요도 없어.

There's no need to think about it.

Sample Sentences

갈 필요도 없어.

There's no need to go.

저 사람 말 들을 필요도 없어.

There's no need to listen to that person.

Exercises

1. There's no need to check. (to check = 확인하다)

   ……›

2. There's no need to answer the phone. (to answer the phone = 전화 받다)

   ……›

Answer Key

1. 확인할 필요도 없어. *2.* 전화 받을 필요도 없어.

Applied Patterns

VERB + -(으)ㄹ 필요 없어

→ 생각할 필요 없어.

There's no need to think about it.

*Even if you drop the -도 after 필요, the general meaning of the sentence doesn't change. However, by adding -도, you can emphasize the meaning that you don't "even" have to think about something.

VERB + -(으)ㄹ 필요도 없어요 formal

→ 생각할 필요도 없어요.

There's no need to think about it.

Pattern 3.

SUBJECT + -은/는 NOUN + -이자 NOUN + -(이)야 casual

SUBJECT is NOUN and also NOUN (at the same time).

Sentence Used in the Dialogue

넌 내 베스트 프렌드이자 내 남동생이야.

You are my best friend and also my younger brother (at the same time).

Sample Sentences

이건 내 카메라이자 mp3야.

This is my camera and also my mp3 player (at the same time).

내 딸은 내 친구이자 내 보물이야.

My daughter is my friend and also my treasure (at the same time).

Exercises

1. Today is my birthday and my sister's birthday (at the same time). (today = 오늘, my birthday = 내 생일, my sister's birthday = 내 여동생의 생일)

   ……〉

2. She is a professor and a writer (at the same time). (she = 그녀, professor = 교수, writer = 작가)

   ……〉

Answer Key
1. 오늘은 내 생일이자 내 여동생의 생일이야. *2.* 그녀는 교수이자 작가야.

Applied Patterns

SUBJECT + -은/는 NOUN + -이자 NOUN + -이기도 해

→ 넌 내 베스트 프렌드이자 내 남동생이기도 해.
You are my best friend and also my younger brother (at the same time).

*If you just use the structure "A + -이자 + B", the meaning of the subject being both A and B at the same time is very clear, but -이기도 해 adds to the meaning that it is "also" B.

SUBJECT + -은/는 NOUN + -이면서 또 NOUN + -(이)야

→ 넌 내 베스트 프렌드이면서 또 내 남동생이야.
You are my best friend and at the same time, you're also my younger brother.

*또 literally means "again" but here, it means "also".

아까 부탁했던 자료는 구해 봤어?

Did you try and look for the data that I asked you for?

•

Overtime Work

Dialogue in Korean

수인: 아... 연말에 야근이라니 정말 힘 빠지네.

예지: 그러게. 다른 팀 사람들은 다 송년회 한다고 밖에서 한잔하고 있을 텐데 말이야.

수인: 그래도 우리는 이 기간만 고생하면 크게 바쁠 일이 없잖아.

예지: 하긴 그래. 연말하고 연초가 제일 고달프지.

수인: 맞아. 아, 그나저나... 아까 부탁했던 자료는 구해 봤어?

예지: 응. 생각보다 양이 많더라고. 자료 뽑는 데도 시간 엄청 걸렸어. 네 책상 위에 뒀어.

수인: 오, 고마워. 나는 이제 그 자료 가지고 보고서 써야 해.

예지: 그래, 고생해라. 나도 보고서 쓰러 가야겠다.

수인: 근데 너 저녁 먹었어?

예지: 아니, 오늘 하루 회의만 다섯 번 했어. 그것도 오후에만.

수인: 나랑 똑같네. 밥 먹을 시간도 없었겠다.

예지: 그렇지 뭐. 아이고, 우리도 뭐 먹을 거 사서 송년회 기분이나 한번 낼까?

수인: 치킨 어때?

English Translation

Su-in: We have to work over time until the year end. It's so depressing.

Ye-ji: Yeah. People on other teams are probably having drinks at their year-end parties.

Su-in: But once we make it through this period, we won't have anything else to keep us too busy.

Ye-ji: Well, that's right. We always have the hardest time at the end of the year and in the beginning of the year.

Su-in: That's right. By the way... did you try and look for the data that I asked you for?

Ye-ji: Yeah. It turns out it was a bigger volume than I thought. It took me a long time just to print it out. I put it on your desk.

Su-in: Oh, thanks. I need to write a report using that data now.

Ye-ji: Okay. Good luck. I've got to go and write a report too.

Su-in: By the way, did you have dinner?

Ye-ji: No. I had about five meetings today. Just in the afternoon alone.

Su-in: The same for me. I guess you didn't even have time to eat.

Ye-ji: Yeah, that's right. How about we buy something to eat and enjoy the year-end party atmosphere?

Su-in: How about chicken?

예지: 안 돼. 치킨 먹으면 맥주 생각나서 보고서 못 쓸 것 같아. 우리 회사 앞에 포장마차에서 하는 떡볶이하고 튀김 먹자.

수인: 순대는 왜 빼먹냐?

예지: 그래. 너네 팀은 누구 남아 있어?

수인: 우리는 규호 씨하고 선화 씨 있어.

예지: 잘됐네. 우리 팀은 나밖에 없으니까 다 같이 분식 먹자고 얘기해 봐.

수인: 응. 선화 씨는 아까 저녁 먹으러 가던 것 같던데...

예지: 그래? 배고픈 사람끼리만 가서 간단하게 먹지 뭐.

수인: 응. 참, 과장님 이따가 오시는데 지금 몇 시지?

예지: 지금 7시 반. 언제 오신대?

수인: 8시 30분쯤에 오신다고 하셨거든. 밖에서 회의하시고 오시는 길인데 차가 좀 막히나 봐.

예지: 그렇구나. 그럼 오시기 전에 다 먹을 수 있겠다.

수인: 그럼 분식 먹고 입가심 겸 카페에 들렀다 오자. 과장님이 아마 커피 부탁할 것 같아서.

예지: 좋아. 그럼 팀원들 데리고 나와.

Ye-ji: No. If I eat chicken, I feel like I won't be able to write the report because I will crave beer. Let's eat some tteokbokki and twigim that are sold in the cart bar in front of our office building.

Su-in: Why did you leave out blood sausages?

Ye-ji: Okay. Who on your team is remaining?

Su-in: On my team, Gyu-ho and Seon-hwa are in the office.

Ye-ji: Good. On my team, it's just me, so why don't you ask them if they want to eat some fast food with us.

Su-in: Sure. But it seemed like Seon-hwa was going out to have dinner earlier.

Ye-ji: Really? Then let's just go and eat something simple just among those who are hungry.

Su-in: Yeah. By the way, the section manager will be coming later. What time is it now?

Ye-ji: It's 7:30. When did he say he will come?

Su-in: He said he would come around 8:30. He'll be on his way back after having a meeting outside, and apparently the traffic is a bit bad.

Ye-ji: Okay. Then we'll be able to eat everything before he arrives.

Su-in: Then after eating this food, let's stop by a café for some dessert. I think the section manager will probably ask me to get coffee for him there.

Ye-ji: Sounds good. Then go get your team members.

Vocabulary

연말	year-end	두다	to put, to place
야근	working overtime, working late	먹을 거	something to eat
힘(이) 빠지다	to feel like one is losing energy out of disappointment or frustration	기분 내다	to create a suitable atmosphere
송년회	year-end party	포장마차	cart bar
한잔하다	to have a drink	빼먹다	to omit, to leave out, to forget
고생하다	to have a hard time, to suffer	남아 있다	to remain, to be left
크게	greatly, largely, highly, loudly	다 같이	all together
연초	the beginning of the year	간단하다	to be simple
고달프다	to be tired out, to be exhausted	이따가	later, after a while
아까	a little while ago	오는 길	one's way to
부탁하다	to request, to ask	차가 막히다	traffic is bad
구하다	to look for, to seek, to get	입가심	rinsing one's mouth out, taking away the aftertaste
양	quantity	들르다	to stop by
뽑다	to print out	아마	probably
엄청나게	tremendously, very	데리고 나오다	to bring out

Pattern Practice

Study these three grammar patterns that were used in the dialogue and practice!

Pattern I.

VERB + -(으)러 가야겠다 casual

I should go and VERB.

Sentence Used in the Dialogue

나도 보고서 쓰러 가야겠다.

I should go and write my report, too.

Sample Sentences

이제 일하러 가야겠다.

I should go and work now.

밥 먹으러 가야겠다.

I should go and eat.

Exercises

1. I should go and meet my friends. (to meet = 만나다, my friends = 친구들)

……〉

2. I should go and sleep. (to go to bed = 자다)

……〉

Answer Key

1. 친구들 만나러 가야겠다. *2.* 자러 가야겠다.

Applied Patterns

VERB + -(으)러 가야 돼

→ 나도 보고서 쓰러 가야 돼.

I should go and write my report, too.

*-아/어/여 돼 is the most common way to say you should do something in casual language. When you say -야겠다, the translated meaning is the same but it has the feeling that you are "assuming" that it's the right thing to do.

VERB + -(으)러 가야겠어요 formal

→ 저도 보고서 쓰러 가야겠어요.

I should go and write my report, too.

*The meaning is the same as 가야겠다, except changing 나 to 저 and using the -어요 ending makes it more formal.

Pattern 2.

VERB + -(으)ㄹ 시간도 없었겠다 casual

I guess you didn't even have time to VERB.

Sentence Used in the Dialogue

밥 먹을 시간도 없었겠다.

I guess you didn't even have time to eat.

Sample Sentences

일할 시간도 없었겠다.

I guess you didn't even have time to work.

잘 시간도 없었겠다.

I guess you didn't even have time to sleep.

Exercises

1. I guess you didn't even have time to drink coffee. (to drink coffee = 커피 마시다)

 ······>

2. I guess you didn't even have time to go home. (to go home = 집에 가다)

 ······>

Answer Key

1. 커피 마실 시간도 없었겠다. *2.* 집에 갈 시간도 없었겠다.

Applied Patterns

VERB + -(으)ㄹ 시간도 없었지?

→ 밥 먹을 시간도 없었지?

You didn't even have time to eat, right?

VERB + -(으)ㄹ 시간도 없었을 것 같아

→ 밥 먹을 시간도 없었을 것 같아.

I guess you didn't even have time to eat.

*것 같아 is the most common way to say "I think" and -겠다 adds the feeling of "assumption" to it.

Pattern 3.

언제 VERB + -(느)ㄴ대? casual

When did (SUBJECT) say (SUBJECT) will VERB?

Sentence Used in the Dialogue

언제 오신대?

When did he say he'll come?

Sample Sentences

언제 말한대?

When did she say she will tell us?

언제 결혼한대?

When did he say he'll get married?

Exercises

1. When did he say it'll be finished? (to be finished = 끝나다)

······>

2. When did she say she'll come back? (to come back = 돌아오다)

······>

Answer Key

1. 언제 끝난대? *2.* 언제 돌아온대?

Applied Patterns

언제 VERB + -겠대?

→ 언제 오시겠대?

When did he say he'll come?

*-겠대 is short for -겠다고 (말)해? and it basically has the same meaning as -(느)ㄴ대? which is short for -(느)ㄴ다고 해? Both of these expressions are used when you want to ask about what someone else said.

언제 VERB + -(느)ㄴ대요? formal

→ 언제 오신대요?

When did he say he'll come?

다른 전달 사항 있나?

Anything else to update on?

Meeting

Dialogue in Korean

팀장: 이번 주 안건들은 뭐가 있나?

최 대리: 네. 여기 있습니다.

팀장: 그래. 먼저, 지난달부터 기획 2팀과 같이 진행해 왔던 프로젝트는 진행 상황이 어떤가?

성 대리: 네. 현재 전략 회의는 마친 상태입니다. 이번 주부터 본격적으로 시장 조사에 들어갔습니다.

팀장: 기획 2팀하고 같이 하는 업무는 처음인가?

성 대리: 네, 처음이에요.

팀장: 아직까지 애로 사항은 없고?

성 대리: 네, 아직 없습니다.

팀장: 그래. 좋네. 이 과장, 이 건은 아직도 진행이 더딘가?

이 과장: 네. 그쪽 거래처 사정이 많이 안 좋아서 잠정 중단됐습니다.

팀장: 괜찮아질 기미가 안 보이나?

이 과장: 네. 가까운 미래에는 좀 힘들 것 같습니다.

팀장: 알겠네. 그럼 이 과장이 맡아서 알아서 처리해 주고.

English Translation

Team Leader: What are the agendas for this week?

Mr. Choi (employee): Yes, here they are.

Team Leader: Okay. First of all, for the project that you've been working on with the Planning Team 2 since last month, how is that going?

Mr. Seong (employee): Yes, so far, we've finished the strategy meeting, and we've started working on the market research this week.

Team Leader: Is it your first time working with Planning Team 2?

Mr. Seong (employee): Yes, it's my first time.

Team Leader: No problems so far?

Mr. Seong (employee): No, no problems so far.

Team Leader: Okay. Good. Mr. Lee, is the processing of this item still slow?

Mr. Lee (Section Chief): Yes. The situation on our business partner's side is not going well so the processing has been temporarily suspended.

Team Leader: Are there no signs of improvement?

Mr. Lee (Section Chief): No. Not likely in the near future.

Team Leader: I understand. Then, Mr. Lee, please decide what to do and take care of it.

이 과장: 네. 알겠습니다.

팀장: 성 대리, 저번 주에 출장 다녀왔지?

성 대리: 네. 다녀왔어요.

팀장: 보고서 올렸나?

성 대리: 아직이요. 오늘 안에 올리도록 하겠습니다.

팀장: 알겠네. 오늘 내가 조금 일찍 퇴근해야 되니까 서두르게. 다른 사람들도 결제 올릴 거 있으면 서두르도록 하세요.

성 대리, 최 대리: 네, 알겠습니다.

팀장: 다른 전달 사항 있나?

최 대리: 아, 네. 총무팀에서 마우스랑 키보드 새로 구비했다고 필요한 분들은 신청하라고 하십니다.

성 대리: 직접 가서 신청하면 되나요?

최 대리: 아, 아니요. 저한테 말해 주시면 제가 취합해서 전달하도록 하겠습니다.

Mr. Lee (Section Chief): Okay. I got it.

Team Leader: Mr. Seong, you went on your business trip last week, right?

Mr. Seong (employee): Yes, that's right.

Team Leader: Did you submit your report?

Mr. Seong (employee): Not yet. I will submit it by today.

Team Leader: Okay. I have to leave work a little early today, so be quick. Also, if any of you have documents that need to be approved, please hurry up.

Mr. Seong, Mr. Choi (employee): Yes, sir.

Team Leader: Anything else to update on?

Mr. Choi (employee): Oh, yes, the general affairs team said they bought new mice and keyboards. They say that you should apply for them if you need them.

Mr. Seong (employee): You just go there and apply?

Mr. Choi (employee): Oh, no. You can tell me, and I will gather the requests and let them know.

Vocabulary

안건	agenda
진행	progress
현재	current, present
전략	strategy
마치	to finish
상태	condition, state, situation
본격적으로	in full scale, in earnest, actively
시장 조사	market research
애로 사항	difficulties
더디다	to be slow
거래처	business partner
사정	situation, circumstance
잠정	tentative
중단되다	to stop, to be discontinued
기미가 보이다	to show signs of
가깝다	to be close
맡다	to take care of, to take charge of
알아서 처리하다	to handle something on one's own
출장	business trip
(보고서) 올리다	to submit (a report)
서두르다	to hurry
결제	payment
전달 사항	message to be delivered
총무팀	general affairs team
새로	newly, anew
구비하다	to be equipped
신청하다	to apply for
직접	directly, in person
취합하다	to collect, to combine
전달하다	to convey

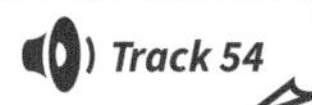

Pattern Practice

Study these three grammar patterns that were used in the dialogue and practice!

Pattern I.

VERB/ADJECTIVE + -(으)ㄹ 것 같습니다 formal

I think (SUBJECT) will VERB / be ADJECTIVE.

Sentence Used in the Dialogue

가까운 미래에는 좀 힘들 것 같습니다.

I think it will be impossible in the near future.

Sample Sentences

오늘까지 끝낼 수 있을 것 같습니다.

I think I will be able to finish it by today.

내일 가야 할 것 같습니다.

I think I will have to go tomorrow.

Exercises

1. I think I will be able to do it. (I = 제가, be able to do it = 할 수 있다)

······〉

2. I think I will be busy tomorrow. (to be busy = 바쁘다, tomorrow = 내일)

······〉

Answer Key

1. 제가 할 수 있을 것 같습니다. 2. 내일 바쁠 것 같습니다.

Applied Patterns

VERB/ADJECTIVE + -(으)ㄹ 것 같아요

→ 가까운 미래에는 좀 힘들 것 같아요.
I think it will be impossible in the near future.

*같아요 has the same meaning as 같습니다, but is slightly less formal.

VERB/ADJECTIVE + -(으)ㄹ 것으로 생각됩니다

→ 가까운 미래에는 좀 힘들 것으로 생각됩니다.
I think it will be impossible in the near future.

*If you say 생각됩니다 instead of -것 같아요, it makes the speech much less direct and therefore a lot more formal.

Pattern 2.

VERB + -도록 하겠습니다 formal

I/We will VERB.

Sentence Used in the Dialogue

오늘 안에 올리도록 하겠습니다.

I will submit it by today.

Sample Sentences

다시 연락 드리도록 하겠습니다.

I will contact you again.

지금 보고서 쓰도록 하겠습니다.

I will write a report now.

Exercises

1. We will refund it. (to refund = 환불해 드리다)

    ......〉

2. I will arrive by 3PM. (to arrive = 도착하다, by 3PM = 3시까지)

    ......〉

Answer Key

1. 환불해 드리도록 하겠습니다. *2. 3*시까지 도착하도록 하겠습니다.

Applied Patterns

VERB + -겠습니다

→ 오늘 안에 올리겠습니다.

I will submit it by today.

*-겠습니다 is a formal way of saying, "I will + do something" but not as formal as -도록 하겠습니다.

VERB + -(으)ㄹ게요

→ 오늘 안에 올릴게요.
I will submit it by today.

*-(으)ㄹ게요 is still formal and polite, but much more casual than -도록 하겠습니다 or -겠습니다.

Pattern 3.

VERB + -(으)라고 하십니다 formal

SUBJECT say(s) that (someone) should VERB.

Sentence Used in the Dialogue

필요한 분들은 신청하라고 하십니다.

They say that you should apply for them if you need them.

Sample Sentences

팀장님께서 보고서 오늘까지 제출하라고 하십니다.
The team manager says that we should submit the report by today.

빨리 촬영하라고 하십니다.
He says that we should film quickly.

Exercises

1. He says you should finish it by today. (to finish = 끝내다, by today = 오늘 안에)

······>

2. He says we should come to eat. (to come to eat = 밥 먹으러 오다)

······>

Answer Key

1. 오늘 안에 끝내라고 하십니다. *2.* 밥 먹으러 오라고 하십니다.

Applied Patterns

VERB + -(으)라고 하시네요

→ 필요한 분들은 신청하라고 하시네요.

They say that you should apply for them if you need them.

*The -네- suffix is often used when you are noticing something and acknowledging it or conveying the information.

VERB + -(으)라고 하셨어요

→ 필요한 분들은 신청하라고 하셨어요.

They said that you should apply for them if you need them.

*-셨어요 is still very formal, but not as formal as -셨습니다.

김 대리 한 잔 해.

Mr. Kim, I'll pour you a drink.

Company Dinner

Dialogue in Korean

팀장: 자, 자, 주목! 엊그제 정 대리 아버님 환갑이셨으니까 우리 오늘 회식 합시다!

모두: 아...

팀장: 안 되는 사람 있나?

이 대리: 없습니다!

유 사원: 저기 저... 전 오늘 선약이 있어서...

팀장: 음... 급한 건가?

유 사원: 아... 급한 건 아니지만 예전부터 해 놓은 약속...

팀장: 급한 거 아니면 참석하지. 팀 식구들이 다 참석하는데 신입 사원이 개인 사정으로 빠지려고?

유 사원: 아, 네...

김 대리: 회사가 다 그런 거야.

(화장실 문 닫는 소리)

김 대리: 아니, 정 대리네 아버님 환갑인데 도대체 왜 우리가 회식을 하는 거야?

이 대리: 이러다 사돈의 팔촌 생일날에도 회식하자고 하겠어.

English Translation

Team Leader: Can I have everybody's attention? It was the 60th birthday of Mr. Jeong's father the other day, so let's have a company dinner today!

Everyone: Uh...

Team Leader: Is there anybody who can't make it?

Ms. Lee (employee): No one.

Mr. Yu (employee): Um... I have some previous engagement.

Team Leader: Hmm... Is it urgent?

Mr. Yu (employee): It's not urgent but I made that arrangement a long time ago...

Team Leader: If it's not urgent, come and join us. Everybody on the team is joining. You're a rookie employee and you are not going to join because of personal matters?!

Mr. Yu (employee): Oh, I see...

Mr. Kim (employee): That's what company life is like.

(Bathroom door closing)

Mr. Kim (employee): I mean, it's Mr. Jeong's father's 60th birthday, so why do we have to have a company dinner?

Ms. Lee (employee): At this rate, he might suggest having a company dinner on the birthday of a distant relative of his in-law.

김 대리: 에휴... 뭐 별수 있나. 가자고 하면 가야지.

이 대리: 나는 오늘 우리 애 생일이라 일찍 들어가야 되는데 남편이랑 또 싸우게 생겼네. 에휴.

김 대리: 눈치 봐서 일찍 들어가야지 뭐.

(회식 장소)

팀장: 자, 자. 한 잔씩들 해. 김 대리 한 잔 해.

김 대리: 네. 감사합니다.

팀장: 아 역시 우리 팀은 정말 가족같아. 우리가 이렇게 지낼 수 있는 건 항상 가족같이 똘똘 뭉쳐서 그런 거야. 안 그런가?

이 대리: 네, 맞습니다 팀장님.

팀장: 김 대리는 어떻게 생각하나?

김 대리: 네, 저도 그렇게 생각해요.

팀장: 그래. 팀이라는 건 이렇게 다 일심동체가 돼야 하는 거야. 허허. 우리 팀이 이렇게 가족같이 화목하게 지내니 기분이 좋구만. 한 잔들 하지. 위하여!

Mr. Kim (employee): Phew... what can we do? If he tells us to, we have to go.

Ms. Lee (employee): I am supposed to go home early today because it's our kid's birthday... I guess I'll have another fight with my husband. Phew...

Mr. Kim (employee): Well, you know, you'll just have to read the atmosphere and then go home early when you can.

(At the company dinner venue)

Team Leader: Come on, let's all have a glass. Mr. Kim, I'll pour you a drink.

Mr. Kim (employee): Yes, thank you.

Team Leader: As always, our team is really like a family. The reason we can get along like this is because we always get together like a family. Don't you think?

Ms. Lee (employee): Yes, that's right, sir.

Team Leader: What do you think, Mr. Kim?

Mr. Kim (employee): Yes, I think so too.

Team Leader: Yes. Teams are supposed to act with one heart and one mind like this. Haha. I'm happy that our team gets along harmoniously like a family. Let's all have a drink. Cheers!

Vocabulary

Track 56

주목	attention	사돈	family-in-law
엊그제	a couple of days ago, a day or two ago	팔촌	third cousin
아버님	someone else's father (honorific)	생일날	birthday
환갑	one's 60th birthday	남편	husband
회식	get-together, work-related dinner, company dinner	싸우다	to fight, to argue
선약	previous engagement	눈치 보다	to read the atmosphere, to be cautious of other people's reactions
급하다	to be urgent	가족	family
예전부터	from a long time ago, since forever	지내다	to spend
약속	engagement, plan	똘똘	onomatopoeia for gathering tightly together
참석하다	to participate	뭉치다	to gather
신입 사원	new employee	맞다	to be right
개인	personal, individual	생각하다	to think
사정	situation, circumstance	일심동체	(idiom) one mind, one body
빠지다	to be omitted, to not be included	화목하다	to be harmonious (family), to be on good terms
도대체	(interrogative +) on earth, in the world	기분이 좋다	to feel good, to feel happy

Pattern Practice

Study these three grammar patterns that were used in the dialogue and practice!

Pattern I.

VERB + -(으)려고? casual

You are going to VERB?!

Sentence Used in the Dialogue

신입 사원이 개인 사정으로 빠지려고?

You're a rookie employee and you are not going to join because of personal matters?!

Sample Sentences

벌써 가려고?

You are going to go already?!

휴대폰 새로 사려고?

You are going to buy a new phone?!

Exercises

1. You are going to come here?! (to come = 오다, here = 여기)

   ……〉

2. You are going to eat all of this?! (to eat them all = 이거 다 먹다)

   ……〉

Answer Key

1. 여기 오려고? *2.* 이거 다 먹으려고?

Applied Patterns

VERB + -(으)ㄹ 거야?

→ 신입 사원이 개인 사정으로 빠질 거야?

You're a rookie employee and you are not going to join because of personal matters?

*-(으)려고? is one way to say "you plan to ...?" or "you intend to ...?" and -(으)ㄹ 거야? is a very neutral way to say "are you going to ...?"

VERB + -(으)려고 해?

→ 신입 사원이 개인 사정으로 빠지려고 해?

You're a rookie employee and you are not going to join because of personal matters?

*Since -(으)려고? is basically a shortened form of -(으)려고 해?, the meaning of both sentences are exactly the same.

Pattern 2.

VERB + -아/어/여야지 뭐 casual

Well, you know, SUBJECT will just have to VERB.

Sentence Used in the Dialogue

눈치 봐서 일찍 들어가야지 뭐.

Well, you know, you will just have to read the atmosphere and then go home early when you can.

Sample Sentences

그냥 해야지 뭐.

Well, you know, I will just have to do it.

밤 새워야지 뭐.

Well, you know, I will just have to stay up all night and do it.

Exercises

1. Well, you know, I will just have to wear this. (to wear = 입다, this = 이거)

……〉

2. Well, you know, I will just have to use this. (to use = 쓰다)

……〉

Answer Key

1. 이거 입어야지 뭐. *2.* 이거 써야지 뭐.

Applied Patterns

그냥 VERB + -아/어/여야지 뭐

→ 그냥 눈치 봐서 일찍 들어가야지 뭐.

Well, you know, you will just have to read the atmosphere and then go home early.

*By adding 그냥, which means "just", it emphasizes the feeling that the choice is limited.

VERB + -아/어/여야지 뭐, 별 수 없지

→ 눈치 봐서 일찍 들어가야지 뭐, 별 수 없지.

Well, you know, you will just have to read the atmosphere and then go home early; you can't help it.

*수 here means "ways", "ideas", or "possibilities", so 별 수 없지 means "there isn't any particular way to do it". More naturally translated, 별 수 없지 means that you can't help it.

Pattern 3.

VERB/NOUN + -(으/이)니까 VERB + -(으)ㅂ시다 formal

Since..., let's VERB.

Sentence Used in the Dialogue

엊그제 정 대리 아버님 환갑이셨으니까 우리 오늘 회식합시다.

It was the 60th birthday of Mr. Jeong's father the other day, so let's have a company dinner today!

Sample Sentences

오늘 유정이 생일이니까 파티합시다.

Since it's Youjeong's birthday, let's have a party.

내일 비 오니까 운동회 취소합시다.

Since it'll rain tomorrow, let's cancel the sports day.

Exercises

1. Since we have consecutive holidays next week, let's go on a trip. (consecutive holidays = 연휴, next week = 다음 주, to go on a trip = 여행가다)

......〉

2. Since Hyunwoo is not here yet, let's wait a little bit more. (to be not here yet = 아직 안 오다, to wait = 기다리다, a little bit more = 조금만 더)

......〉

Answer Key

1. 다음 주 연휴니까 여행갑시다. *2.* 현우가 아직 안 왔으니까 조금만 더 기다립시다.

Applied Patterns

VERB/NOUN + -(으/이)니까 VERB + -(으)ㄹ까요?

→ 엊그제 정 대리 아버님 환갑이셨으니까 우리 오늘 회식할까요?

Shall we have a company dinner since it was the 60th birthday of Mr. Jeong's father the other day?

VERB/NOUN + -(으/이)니까 VERB + -자 casual

→ 엊그제 정 대리 아버님 환갑이셨으니까 우리 오늘 회식하자.

Let's have a company dinner since it was the 60th birthday of Mr. Jeong's father the other day.

너 수강 신청 다 했어?

Did you finish registering for your classes?

Class

Dialogue in Korean

수영: 현철아, 너 수강 신청 다 했어?

현철: 응. 다 했지. 겨우 20학점 채웠다. 너는?

수영: 나는 18학점. 듣고 싶은 수업이 있었는데 금방 정원이 다 차 버려서 못 들어갔어.

현철: 무슨 수업 들으려고 했는데?

수영: 영어 발달사.

현철: 아, 오건영 교수님 수업이지?

수영: 응. 수업도 재밌고, 참여도만 좋으면 학점도 좋게 주신다고 하더라고.

현철: 하긴 그건 그래.

수영: 어! 너 그 수업 들었었어? 어땠어?

현철: 응. 지난 학기에 들었어. 그룹 발표 과제가 있어서 그게 좀 어렵긴 했는데 뭔가 많이 배운 것 같아.

수영: 너 학점은 얼마나 나왔어?

현철: 나 A 받았지. 시험은 그렇게 잘 보진 않았는데, 네 말대로 내가 이것저것 많이 참여했었거든. 그래서 학점을 좀 후하게 주신 것 같아. 나, 애들 앞에서 노래도 불렀어. 장난 아니었어.

수영: 그렇구나. 그 수업을 들어야 되는데... 어떡하지?

English Translation

Su-yeong: Hyeon-cheol, did you finish registering for your classes?

Hyeon-cheol: Yes, I've finished. I barely managed to fill 20 credits. You?

Su-yeong: I am taking 18 credits. There was a class I wanted to take but it filled up quickly so I couldn't get in.

Hyeon-cheol: What class did you want to take?

Su-yeong: It was History of the Development of English.

Hyeon-cheol: Oh, that's the class by Professor Geon-yeong Oh, right?

Su-yeong: Yeah, the class is fun, and I heard that he gives good grades if you just participate a lot.

Hyeon-cheol: Yeah, it's kind of true.

Su-yeong: Oh, you took that class? How was it?

Hyeon-cheol: Yeah, I took it last semester. There were some group project assignments so that was a bit hard, but I think I kind of learned a lot.

Su-yeong: What grade did you get?

Hyeon-cheol: I got an A. I didn't really do that well on the test, but like you said, I participated a lot in this and that. So I think he was generous with my grade. I even sang in front of other students. It was crazy.

Su-yeong: I see. I need to take that class... What should I do?

현철: 교수님 따로 찾아뵙고 말씀드리는 건 어때? 혹시 알아? 받아 주실지?

수영: 응. 그래야겠어.

현철: 넌? 이번에 재밌는 수업 들어?

수영: 재밌는 수업? 음... 결혼과 생활이라는 수업 신청했어. 재밌다는 얘기가 많더라고.

현철: 그래? 나도 그 수업 얘기 들었는데 재밌어 보이더라. 소문을 듣기로는, 솔로인 애가 그 수업 듣다가 애인이 생기면 무조건 A+ 준다는 얘기가 있더라고.

수영: 진짜? 연애 잘하는 법 가르쳐 주는 거야? 그럼 정말 좋을 텐데.

현철: 그래. 너도 대학 다닐 때 애인 만들어 봐야 하지 않겠냐.

수영: 그게 말처럼 쉬워야 말이지. 아무튼, 난 이제 집으로 갈래.

현철: 그래. 잘 들어가라. 내일 봐.

Hyeon-cheol: How about visiting the professor and talking to him? Who knows? Maybe he will let you in?

Su-yeong: Yeah, I gotta do that.

Hyeon-cheol: How about you? Any interesting classes you are taking this time?

Su-yeong: Interesting classes? Um... I signed up for a class called "Marriage and Life". I heard a lot of people saying that it's fun.

Hyeon-cheol: Yeah? I heard about that class too and it seems fun. Rumor has it that if you are single and get a girlfriend or boyfriend while taking that class, you will get an A+ no matter what.

Su-yeong: Really? They teach you how to date well? Then it would be really nice.

Hyeon-cheol: Yeah. You need to see someone while you're in college.

Su-yeong: It's easier said than done. Anyway, I'm going to head home now.

Hyeon-cheol: Okay. Bye. See you tomorrow.

Vocabulary

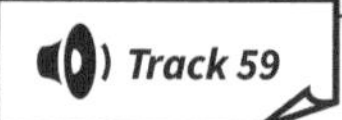

수강	taking a class
신청	application
채우다	to fill
(수업을) 듣다	to take a class
정원	capacity, number limit
차다	to be full of, to be filled with
참여도	level of participation
학점	school credit
주시다	to give (honorific)
학기	semester
발표	presentation
과제	assignment, homework
어렵다	to be hard, to be difficult
참여하다	to participate
후하다	to be generous
노래 부르다	to sing a song
찾아뵙다	to visit (honorific)
말씀드리다	to tell (honorific)
받아 주시다	to accept (honorific)
결혼	wedding
생활	life, living
소문	rumor
듣다	to listen
솔로	single
애인	girlfriend, boyfriend, lover
생기다	to happen, to be formed, to be made
무조건	no matter what, unconditionally
연애	dating, going out with someone
가르쳐 주다	to teach

Pattern Practice

Study these three grammar patterns that were used in the dialogue and practice!

Pattern I.

겨우 VERB + -았/었/였다 casual

I barely managed to VERB.

Sentence Used in the Dialogue

겨우 20학점 채웠다.

I barely managed to fill 20 credits.

Sample Sentences

겨우 막차 탔다.

I barely managed to get on the last bus.

1분 남겨 놓고 겨우 끝냈다.

I barely managed to finish it with just one minute remaining.

Exercises

1. I barely managed to pass the exam. (to pass the exam = 시험에 합격하다)

······〉

2. Due to bad traffic, I barely managed to arrive on time. (due to the traffic = 차가 막혀서, to arrive = 도착하다)

······〉

Answer Key

1. 시험에 겨우 합격했다. *2.* 차가 막혀서 겨우 도착했다.

Applied Patterns

간신히 VERB + -았/었/였다

→ 간신히 20학점 채웠다.

I barely managed to fill 20 credits.

*간신히 means the same as 겨우 in this context, which is "barely managing to do something". 겨우 has other meanings as well, which include "only" or "just".

가까스로 VERB + -았/었/였다

→ 가까스로 20학점 채웠다.

I barely managed to fill 20 credits.

*가까스로 means the same as 간신히.

Pattern 2.

VERB + -는 건 어때? casual

How about VERB-ing?

Sentence Used in the Dialogue

교수님 따로 찾아뵙고 말씀드리는 건 어때?

How about visiting the professor and talking to him?

Sample Sentences

여기서 한국어 공부해 보는 건 어때?

How about trying to study Korean here?

이거 한 번 써 보는 건 어때?

How about trying to use this?

Exercises

1. How about trying to apply here? (to try to apply = 지원해 보다, here = 여기)

……〉

2. How about taking the train? (to go = 가다, by train = 기차 타고)

……〉

Answer Key

1. 여기 지원해 보는 건 어때? *2.* 기차 타고 가는 건 어때?

Applied Patterns

VERB + -는 게 어떨까?

→ 교수님 따로 찾아뵙고 말씀드리는 게 어떨까?

How about visiting the professor and talking to him?

*어때? and 어떨까? basically mean the same thing, but by saying 어떨까?, you are also asking yourself or wondering.

VERB + -는 건 어때요? formal

→ 교수님 따로 찾아뵙고 말씀드리는 건 어때요?
How about visiting the professor and talking to him?

Pattern 3.

NOUN + -(이)라는 NOUN

NOUN called NOUN

Sentence Used in the Dialogue

결혼과 생활이라는 수업 신청했어.

I signed up for a class called "Marriage and Life".

Sample Sentences

또와분식이라는 음식점인데 진짜 맛있어.
It's a restaurant called "Tto-wa-bun-sik" and it's really good.

2호선에 사당이라는 역이 있어.
There's a station called "Sa-dang" on subway line number two.

Exercises

1. It's a movie called "Gun-ham-do". (movie = 영화)

······〉

2. Do you know the brand called Basta? (do you know? = 알아?, brand = 브랜드)

······〉

Answer Key

1. 군함도라는 영화야. *2.* 바스타라는 브랜드 알아?

Applied Patterns

NOUN + -(이)라는 이름의 NOUN

→ 결혼과 생활이라는 이름의 수업 신청했어.
I signed up for a class named "Marriage and Life".

NOUN + -(이)라는 제목의 NOUN

→ 결혼과 생활이라는 제목의 수업 신청했어.
I signed up for a class titled "Marriage and Life".

왜 항상 시험 때가 가까워져서 후회할까?

Why do I always regret not studying in advance when the exam draws near?

•

Exam

Dialogue in Korean

수진: 유희야. 우리 수학 시험 범위 51페이지까지 맞지?

유희: 음... 잠깐만.

수진: 응.

유희: 51페이지? 나는 63페이지라고 써 있는데?

수진: 응? 진짜?

유희: 응. 여기 봐 봐. 5과 63페이지까지.

수진: 헐.

유희: 뭐야. 4과까지만 공부한 거야?

수진: 응... 아, 어떡해. 망했어!

유희: 야, 괜찮아. 이번 주말에 바짝 하면 돼.

수진: 다른 것도 공부할 거 많은데... 전날 밤 새서 벼락치기 해야겠다.

유희: 전날 안 자고 공부한다고?

수진: 응. 그래야지 뭐 어쩌겠어. 아... 정말 바보 같아.

유희: 너 안 자고 할 수 있겠어? 나는 시험 전날 벼락치기 절대 못 해.

수진: 왜?

English Translation

Su-jin: Yu-hee, our math exam will cover up to page 51, right?

Yu-hee: Um, just a second.

Su-jin: Okay.

Yu-hee: Page 51? My note says it's page 63.

Su-jin: Huh? Really?

Yu-hee: Yeah. Look here. Chapter 5, page 63.

Su-jin: Oh my gosh.

Yu-hee: What, you only studied up to chapter 4?

Su-jin: Yeah. Oh, no! I'm screwed!

Yu-hee: Hey, it's okay. You'll just have to study really hard this weekend.

Su-jin: I have a lot of other things to study... I will have to stay up all night and cram for it the night before.

Yu-hee: You are going to study without sleeping the night before?

Su-jin: Yeah, what else can I do? Argh... I feel like such an idiot.

Yu-hee: Will you be able to take the exam without sleeping? I can never cram for a test the day before.

Su-jin: Why?

유희: 하나도 안 자고 가면 그다음 날 항상 졸아.

수진: 아, 진짜? 그럼 넌 시험 전날 밤 새면 안 되겠네.

유희: 어. 난 그래서 시험 전날 항상 푹 자.

수진: 그럼 다음 날 컨디션은 참 좋겠다.

유희: 응, 그러니까. 그래서 미리미리 하는 수밖에 없어.

수진: 아... 나도 미리미리 좀 해 놓을걸. 왜 항상 시험 때가 가까워져서 후회할까?

유희: 그러게. 평소에는 시험 때 되면 벼락치기 할 생각만 하고, 막상 시험 때가 되면 평소에 공부 안 한 걸 후회하게 돼.

수진: 맞아. 진짜 그런 것 같아. 그래도 다음 시험은 꼭 평소에 준비해 놓을 거야!

Yu-hee: If I don't sleep at all the night before, I always doze off the next day.

Su-jin: Oh, really? Then I guess you shouldn't stay up all night the day before an exam.

Yu-hee: Yeah. So I always sleep well the day before an exam.

Su-jin: Then the next day, you must feel really good.

Yu-hee: Yes, that's what I'm saying. So I just have to study in advance.

Su-jin: Argh... I should have studied in advance, too. Why do I always regret not studying in advance when the exam draws near?

Yu-hee: I know, right? Usually, I just think of cramming for the exam, and when the exam period actually comes around, I regret not having studied at normal times.

Su-jin: Right. I think it's really like that. But still, for the next exam, I will make sure I prepare in advance.

Vocabulary

수학	math
시험	text, exam
범위	range
잠깐만	just a second
써 있다	to be written
공부하다	to study
괜찮다	to be okay, to be alright
주말	weekend
바짝	intensely, (following) right after, really hard
다른 것	something else, another thing
많다	to be a lot
전날	the previous day
밤 새다	to stay up all night
벼락치기	cramming, hasty preparation
자다	to sleep
바보	fool, idiot
절대	never
졸다	to doze off
좋다	to be good
미리미리	beforehand
가까워지다	to get near
후회하다	to regret
평소	usual times, usually, normally
다음	next
준비하다	to prepare

Pattern Practice

Study these three grammar patterns that were used in the dialogue and practice!

Pattern 1.

괜찮아. VERB + -(으)면 돼 casual

It's okay. (SUBJECT) can just VERB.

Sentence Used in the Dialogue

괜찮아. 이번 주말에 바짝 하면 돼.

It's okay. You can just study really hard this weekend.

Sample Sentences

괜찮아. 내일 많이 자면 돼.

It's okay. I can just sleep a lot tomorrow.

괜찮아. 빨리 끝내면 돼.

It's okay. I can just finish it quickly.

Exercises

1. It's okay. We can just see it next time. (to see it = 보다, next time = 다음에)

······〉

2. It's okay. I can just ask someone else. (to ask another person = 다른 사람한테 물어보다)

······〉

Answer Key

1. 괜찮아. 다음에 보면 돼. *2.* 괜찮아. 다른 사람한테 물어보면 돼.

Applied Patterns

괜찮아. VERB + -(으)면 되지

→ 괜찮아. 이번 주말에 바짝 하면 되지.

It's okay. You can just study really hard this weekend.

*-지 is used when you are confirming a fact or telling the other person what they should already know. It can also be used when reinforcing or correcting what the listener thinks or knows.

괜찮아. VERB + -(으)면 될 거야

→ 괜찮아. 이번 주말에 바짝 하면 될 거야

It's okay. If you just study intensely this weekend, you'll be alright.

Pattern 2.

SUBJECT + -은/는 절대 못 VERB + -아/어/여 casual

SUBJECT can never VERB. / SUBJECT definitely can't VERB.

Sentence Used in the Dialogue

나는 시험 전날 벼락치기 절대 못 해.

I can never cram for a test the day before.

Sample Sentences

나는 그때는 절대 못 가.

I definitely can't go then.

너는 저 남자 절대 못 이겨.

You can never beat him.

Exercises

1. I definitely can't finish this today. (to finish = 끝내다, this = 이거, today = 오늘 안에)

    ......〉

2. I can never meet that person again. (to meet = 만나다, that person = 그 사람, again = 다시)

    ......〉

Answer Key

1. 나는 이거 오늘 안에 절대 못 끝내. *2.* 나는 그 사람 절대 다시 못 만나.

Applied Patterns

SUBJECT + -은/는 절대 못 VERB + -(으)ㄹ 거야

→ 나는 시험 전날 벼락치기 절대 못 할 거야.

I will never be able to cram for a test the day before.

SUBJECT + -은/는 절대로 못 VERB + -아/어/여

→ 나는 시험 전날 벼락치기 절대로 못 해.
I can never cram for a test the day before.

*절대 and 절대로 basically mean the same thing, but 절대로 is stronger than 절대.

Pattern 3.

꼭 VERB + -(으)ㄹ 거야 casual

I will make sure I VERB.

Sentence Used in the Dialogue

다음 시험은 꼭 평소에 준비해 놓을 거야.

I will make sure I prepare in advance.

Sample Sentences

네 결혼식은 꼭 갈 거야.
I will make sure I go to your wedding.

꼭 그 맛집에서 먹을 거야.
I will make sure I eat at that famous restaurant.

Exercises

1. I will make sure I change my phone by tomorrow. (to change my phone 휴대폰 바꾸다, by tomorrow = 내일까지)

   ......〉

2. I will make sure I meet that person. (to meet that person = 그 사람 만나다)

……›

Answer Key
1. 내일까지 꼭 휴대폰 바꿀 거야. *2.* 꼭 그 사람 만날 거야.

Applied Patterns

꼭 VERB + -(으)ㄹ게

→ 다음 시험은 꼭 평소에 준비해 놓을게.
I will make sure I prepare in advance.

*-(으)ㄹ 거야 is commonly used to express plain future tense, while -(으)ㄹ게 is commonly used to show intention.

꼭 VERB + -(으)ㄹ 거예요 formal

→ 다음 시험은 꼭 평소에 준비해 놓을 거예요.
I will make sure I prepare in advance.

*-(으)ㄹ 거예요 is more formal than -(으)ㄹ 거야.

떡볶이 생각나서 왔어요.

We felt like eating tteokbokki so we came.

Restaurant

원조 떡볶이

Dialogue in Korean

주희: 아... 춥다. 춥다. 얼른 밥 먹으러 가자. 뭐 먹을까?

윤미: 음... 난 아무거나!

희정: 나도 아무거나 상관 없어.

주희: 너네 그럴 줄 알았다. 그럼 추운데 우동이나 먹으러 갈까?

윤미: 오늘 점심에 먹었어.

주희: 그럼 파스타 먹으러 가자.

희정: 어우, 느끼해. 싫어.

주희: 아오! 진짜 내 이것들을 그냥!

윤미: 우리 오랜만에 거기 갈까? 우리 학교 다닐 때 매일 갔던 데?

주희: 떡볶이?

희정: 좋아!

주희: 콜!

아저씨: 어서 오세요!

주희: 안녕하세요, 아저씨!

아저씨: 응. 어서들 와. 왜 이렇게 오랜만에 왔어?

English Translation

Ju-hee: It's cold! Let's hurry up and go eat. What shall we eat?

Yun-mi: Um, I'm good with anything.

Hui-jeong: I'm up for anything too.

Ju-hee: I thought you guys would say that. Then, since it's cold, how about we go eat some udon noodles?

Yun-mi: I had them for lunch.

Ju-hee: Then let's go eat pasta.

Hui-jeong: Oh no. It's too greasy. No.

Ju-hee: Come on, you guys. Argh.

Yun-mi: How about we go to a place that we haven't been in a while. The place we used to go to every day when we were in school.

Ju-hee: Tteokbokki?

Hui-jeong: Sounds good!

Ju-hee: Let's do it.

Clerk: Welcome.

Ju-hee: Hi!

Clerk: Hey, welcome, come in. I haven't seen you guys in a while.

윤미: 바쁘게 살다 보니까 그렇게 되네요. 떡볶이 생각나서 왔어요.

아저씨: 그래, 잘 왔어. 뭐 줄까?

주희: 떡볶이 하나, 순대 하나, 튀김 다섯 개, 아니, 여섯 개 주세요.

아저씨: 응. 그래.

희정: 떡볶이 맵게 해 주세요. 아주 맵게요!

윤미: 야. 안 돼! 나 매운 거 먹으면 속 쓰려. 아저씨! 아주 맵게 말고 적당히! 적당히 맵게 해 주세요.

주희: 아, 그리고 파는 빼 주세요!

아저씨: 응, 알지! 파 빼고 적당히 맵고 맛있게 해 줄게. 조금만 기다려!

Yun-mi: Yeah, just busy with life and all. We felt like eating tteokbokki so we came.

Clerk: Glad you came back. What do you want to have?

Ju-hee: One serving of tteokbokki, one (serving of) blood sausage, and five, no, six twigims.

Clerk: Okay.

Hui-jeong: Please make the tteokbokki spicy. Very spicy.

Yun-mi: Hey, no! I get heartburn if I eat spicy food. Don't make it too spicy. Just moderately spicy, please.

Ju-hee: Oh, and leave out the green onions, please.

Clerk: Sure, I know! I'll leave out the green onions and make it moderately spicy and delicious. Just wait for a little bit!

Vocabulary

춥다	to be cold
얼른	quickly
먹으러 가다	to go to eat
아무거나	anything
점심	lunch
느끼하다	to be greasy
싫다	to hate, to dislike
오랜만에	in a long time, after not doing so for a long time
거기	there
학교	school
다니다	to go (to a place regularly), to attend (regularly)
매일	every day
떡볶이	tteokbokki (rice cakes in spicy sauce)
좋다	to be good
오다	to come
바쁘다	to be busy
살다	to live
생각나다	to feel like
순대	blood sausage
튀김	twigim (deep-fried foods)
맵다	to be spicy
아주	very
속 쓰리다	to have an upset stomach, to get heartburn
적당히	properly, appropriately, suitably
빼다	to subtract, to take out
맛있다	to be tasty
조금만	a little bit
기다리다	to wait

Pattern Practice

Study these three grammar patterns that were used in the dialogue and practice!

Pattern I.

얼른 VERB + -(으)러 가자 casual

Let's hurry and go VERB.

Sentence Used in the Dialogue

얼른 밥 먹으러 가자.

Let's hurry up and go eat.

Sample Sentences

얼른 친구들 보러 가자.

Let's hurry and go meet my friends.

얼른 비행기 타러 가자.

Let's hurry and go get on the airplane.

Exercises

1. Let's hurry and go hang out. (to hang out = 놀다)

 ......〉

2. Let's hurry up and go for a walk. (to go for a walk = 산책하다)

 ......〉

Answer Key

1. 얼른 놀러 가자. *2*. 얼른 산책하러 가자.

Applied Patterns

얼른 가서 VERB + -아/어/여자

→ 얼른 가서 밥 먹자.

Let's hurry up and go eat.

빨리 VERB + -(으)러 가자

→ 빨리 밥 먹으러 가자.

Let's hurry up and go eat.

*얼른 and 빨리 both mean "early" or "quickly", but 얼른 is only used in spoken Korean.

Pattern 2.

Someone VERB + -(으)ㄹ 줄 알았다 casual

I knew someone would VERB.

Sentence Used in the Dialogue

너네 그럴 줄 알았다.

I knew you guys would say that.

Sample Sentences

너 오늘 늦을 줄 알았다.

I knew you would be late today.

쟤 넘어질 줄 알았다.

I knew he would fall.

Exercises

1. I knew you would have a stomachache. (to have a stomachache = 배탈나다)

   ……›

2. I knew you would sing that song. (to sing the song = 그 노래 부르다)

   ……›

Answer Key

1. 너 배탈 날 줄 알았다. *2.* 너 그 노래 부를 줄 알았다.

Applied Patterns

Someone VERB + -(으)ㄹ 것 같더라

→ 너네 그럴 것 같더라.

I knew you guys would say that.

*-더라 is a way to talk about one's observation or what seemed like was the case.

Someone VERB + -(으)ㄹ 줄 알았어

→ 너네 그럴 줄 알았어.

I knew you guys would say that.

*알았다 is an exclamation, while 알았어 is in the plain present tense.

Pattern 3.

VERB/ADJECTIVE + -아/어/여서 왔어요 formal

I/We PAST TENSE VERB / was/were ADJECTIVE so I/we came (here).

Sentence Used in the Dialogue

떡볶이 생각나서 왔어요.

We felt like eating tteokbokki so we came.

Sample Sentences

이게 고장 나서 왔어요.

This broke so I came.

강아지 보고 싶어서 왔어요.

We wanted to see the puppy so we came.

Exercises

1. I was bored so I came. (to be bored = 심심하다)

······〉

2. I was hungry so I came. (to be hungry = 배고프다)

······›

Answer Key

1. 심심해서 왔어요. *2*. 배고파서 왔어요.

Applied Patterns

VERB/ADJECTIVE + -길래 왔어요

→ 떡볶이 생각나길래 왔어요.

Since I felt like eating tteokbokki, I came.

*-길래 is used when you are talking about something that happened, and then it became the reason for your reaction or response.

VERB/ADJECTIVE + -아/어/여서 왔어 casual

→ 떡볶이 생각나서 왔어.

I felt like eating tteokbokki so I came.

다진 마늘은 냉동실에 있을 거야.

Minced garlic should be in the freezer.

•

Cooking

Dialogue in Korean

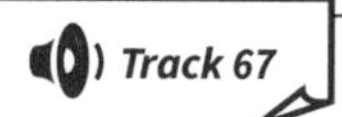

병희: 오늘 저녁은 뭐 해 줄 거야?

윤화: 뭐 먹고 싶은 거 있어?

병희: 우리 돼지고기 있잖아. 그거 구워 먹을까?

윤화: 그냥 구워 먹어?

병희: 아니, 불고기로 만들어서 먹자.

윤화: 좋아. 그럼 우선 양파를 강판에 갈아 놓을래? 그리고 냉장고에 배도 있으니까 배도 같이 갈아 줘.

병희: 응. 얼마나 할까?

윤화: 양파 한 개, 배는 반쪽만 하면 돼.

병희: 알았어. 마늘 다진 거하고 간장도 넣어야 되지?

윤화: 당연하지. 다진 마늘은 냉동실에 있을 거야. 한두 숟갈 정도 떼어서 그릇에 넣어.

병희: 생강도 넣어야 맛있는데...

윤화: 생강 저번 주에 다 썼어. 많이 안 먹어서 상해서 버렸잖아. 생강은 생략.

병희: 알았어.

윤화: 그러고 난 다음에 꿀 한 숟갈 반 넣고, 후추, 참기름 넣어.

English Translation

Byeong-hee: What will you make for dinner today?

Yun-hwa: Is there something that you'd like to eat?

Byeong-hee: You know we have some pork. Shall we grill that?

Yun-hwa: Just grill it?

Byeong-hee: No, let's make some bulgogi with it.

Yun-hwa: Good. Then can you grate some onion with the grater first? And there is a pear in the fridge too, so please grate the pear with it as well.

Byeong-hee: Sure. How much?

Yun-hwa: One onion, and just a piece of pear will be enough.

Byeong-hee: Okay. I have to put in some minced garlic and soy sauce too, right?

Yun-hwa: Of course. Minced garlic should be in the freezer. Take a couple spoonfuls of it and put it into the bowl.

Byeong-hee: We need to add some ginger to make it tasty...

Yun-hwa: We used up all the ginger last week. We weren't eating a lot of it so it went bad and we had to throw it away. Let's skip the ginger.

Byeong-hee: Okay.

Yun-hwa: And then add one and a half spoonfuls of honey, and then add some pepper and sesame oil.

병희: 응. 우리 당근 남은 거 있는데 그것도 넣을까?

윤화: 좋아. 당근 얇게 썰어서 넣어.

병희: 다 넣었어. 이제 막 주무르면 되지?

윤화: 응. 이제 한 1시간 재워 놓고 구워 먹으면 돼.

병희: 엥? 1시간이나 기다려야 해?

윤화: 그래야 맛있어져.

병희: 아... 배고픈데...

Byeong-hee: Yeah. We have some leftover carrots. Shall I put them in too?

Yun-hwa: Good. Cut some thin slices of carrots and add those.

Byeong-hee: I've added them all. Now I just have to mix it all up, right?

Yun-hwa: Yeah. Now let it sit for about an hour, and then we can grill it.

Byeong-hee: Huh? We have to wait an hour?

Yun-hwa: That's how you make it delicious.

Byeong-hee: Argh... I'm hungry...

Vocabulary

저녁	dinner
돼지고기	pork
구워 먹다	to grill and eat
양파	onion
강판	grater
갈다	to grate
냉장고	fridge
배	pear
다지다	to mince
간장	soy sauce
넣다	to put something in, to add
냉동실	freezer
떼다	to take, to remove, to detach
그릇	bowl
생강	ginger
상하다	to go bad, to be damaged
버리다	to throw away
생략	skip
꿀	honey
한 숟갈	one spoon
반	half
후추	black pepper
참기름	sesame oil
당근	carrot
남다	to remain, to be left
얇다	to be thin
썰다	to cut, to chop, to slice
주무르다	to massage, to rub down
재워 놓다	to marinate something
배고프다	to be hungry

Pattern Practice

Study these three grammar patterns that were used in the dialogue and practice!

Pattern I.

VERB + -고 싶은 거 있어? casual

Is there something that you want to/would like to VERB?

Sentence Used in the Dialogue

뭐 먹고 싶은 거 있어?

Is there something that you'd like to eat?

Sample Sentences

뭐 갖고 싶은 거 있어?

Is there something that you want to have?

보고 싶은 거 있어?

Is there anything that you'd like to watch?

Exercises

1. Is there something that you want to drink? (to drink = 마시다)

    ......〉

2. Is there anything that you'd like to do? (to do = 하다)

    ......〉

Answer Key

1. 마시고 싶은 거 있어? *2.* 하고 싶은 거 있어?

Applied Patterns

VERB + -고 싶은 거 없어?

→ 뭐 먹고 싶은 거 없어?

Don't you have anything to eat?

VERB + -고 싶은 거 있어요? formal

→ 뭐 먹고 싶은 거 있어요?

Is there something that you want to eat?

Pattern 2.

VERB + -아/어/여야 되지? casual

(SUBJECT) has/have to VERB, right?

Sentence Used in the Dialogue

간장도 넣어야 되지?

I have to put in some soy sauce too, right?

Sample Sentences

7시까지 가야 되지?

I have to be there by 7, right?

너 지금 점심 먹어야 되지?

You have to have lunch now, right?

Exercises

1. I have to meet that person this Saturday, right? (to meet = 만나다, that person = 그 사람, this Saturday = 이번 주 토요일에)

……〉

2. We have to move this, right? (to move = 옮기다, this = 이거)

……〉

Answer Key

1. 이번주 토요일에 그 사람 만나야 되지?. *2.* 이거 옮겨야 되지?

Applied Patterns

VERB + -아/어/여야지?

→ 간장도 넣어야지?

I have to put in some soy sauce too, right?

*-아/어/여야지? is short for -아/어/여야 하지? or 되지?

VERB + -아/어/여야 하지?

→ 간장도 넣어야 하지?

I have to put in some soy sauce too, right?

*-야 되다 and -야 하다 both mean "to have to" do something.

Pattern 3.

SUBJECT + -은/는 NOUN + -에 있을 거야 casual

SUBJECT should be in/at NOUN.

Sentence Used in the Dialogue

다진 마늘은 냉동실에 있을 거야.

Minced garlic should be in the freezer.

Sample Sentences

주연이는 회사에 있을 거야.

Jooyeon should be at the company.

가위는 서랍 안에 있을 거야.

The scissors should be in the drawer.

Exercises

1. That book should be at the library. (that book = 그 책, to be in a library = 도서관에 있다)

……〉

2. Hyunwoo should be in the U.S. now. (to be in the U.S. = 미국에 있다)

……〉

Answer Key

1. 그 책은 도서관에 있을 거야. *2.* 현우는 지금 미국에 있을 거야.

Applied Patterns

SUBJECT + -은/는 NOUN + -에 있어

→ 다진 마늘은 냉동실에 있어.

Minced garlic is in the freezer.

SUBJECT + -은/는 아마 NOUN + -에 있을 거야

→ 다진 마늘은 아마 냉동실에 있을 거야.

Minced garlic is probably in the freezer.

짜장면도 시킬 수 있지?

I can order black bean noodles too, right?

•

Ordering Delivery

Dialogue in Korean

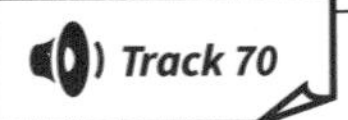

현주: 아, 진짜 배고프다. 우리 점심 뭐 먹을까?

수영: 나도 배고파. 진짜 뭐 먹지? 맛있는 거 먹고 싶다.

현주: 날씨도 추운데, 우리 그냥 뭐 시켜 먹을까? 밖에 나가기 너무 귀찮아.

수영: 그래. 시켜 먹자. 뭐 시키지? 피자? 치킨?

현주: 치킨을 점심으로 먹자고?

수영: 뭐 어때? 아니면 중국집에서 배달시켜 먹을까?

현주: 잠깐만 기다려 봐. 앱으로 한번 찾아볼게. 우와, 종류 진짜 많은데? 떡볶이 같은 분식도 배달해 주네.

수영: 이게 뭐야? 음식 배달시키는 앱도 있어?

현주: 너 아직 이런 앱도 몰라? 아휴... 너 너무 시대에 뒤떨어진 거 아냐?

수영: 야, 집에 쌓여 있는 전단지들 많은데 거기서 골라서 시켜 먹으면 되지. 꼭 앱까지 깔아야 돼?

현주: 됐다, 됐어. 자, 우선 종류를 골라 봐. 한식, 양식, 중국식, 분식?

수영: 무슨 종류가 그렇게 많아. 대충 골라.

현주: 그럼 니가 한번 봐 봐. 엄청 매운 떡볶이도 있네. 이거 시킬까?

English Translation

Hyeon-ju: I'm so hungry. What shall we have for lunch?

Su-yeong: I am hungry too. For real, what should we have? I want to eat something delicious.

Hyeon-ju: The weather is quite cold so how about we just order something for delivery? It's too much hassle to go outside.

Su-yeong: Yeah, let's order delivery. What should we order? Pizza? Chicken?

Hyeon-ju: Chicken for lunch?

Su-yeong: What's wrong with that? Or how about we order delivery from a Chinese restaurant?

Hyeon-ju: Wait a second. I'll look up delivery places on the app. Wow, there is such a wide variety. They deliver instant foods like tteokbokki too.

Su-yeong: What is this? Is there an app for food delivery?

Hyeon-ju: You don't know about these apps yet? (Sigh) You seem so behind the times.

Su-yeong: Come on. I have a pile of delivery menus at home. I can just pick one of them and order. Do I really have to install an app as well?

Hyeon-ju: Forget it. So first choose a category: Korean food, Western food, Chinese food, instant food?

Su-yeong: Why are there so many kinds? Just pick whatever.

Hyeon-ju: Then you take a look. They also have super spicy tteokbokki.

수영: 난 그냥 짜장면 먹을래. 짜장면도 시킬 수 있지?

현주: 맨날 짜장면이야? 다른 것 좀 시켜 먹자.

수영: 그럼 니가 골라. 벌써 12시 다 돼 가잖아. 더 늦게 시키면 배달 시간 엄청 길어진다고. 나 배고파.

현주: 알았어. 알았어. 기다려 봐. 여기가 맛있을 거 같아. 리뷰가 많이 달렸어.

수영: 여보세요. 거기 중국집이죠?

현주: 야! 뭐 해?

수영: 여기 짜장면 한 개랑 탕수육 작은 거 주시고요. 너 뭐 먹을래?

현주: 아, 진짜! 그럼 난 볶음밥.

수영: 볶음밥도 추가해 주세요. 얼마나 걸려요? 30분이요? 빨리 좀 갖다 주세요. 그리고 짬뽕 국물도 좀 주세요. 카드로 결제할게요.

현주: 야, 나 매운 떡볶이 먹고 싶었단 말이야...

Su-yeong: I will just have black bean noodles. I can order black bean noodles too, right?

Hyeon-ju: Don't you eat black bean noodles every day? Let's order something else.

Su-yeong: Then you choose. It's already almost 12 o'clock. If you order later than that, the delivery time will be really long. I am hungry.

Hyeon-ju: Okay, okay. Just wait a bit. I think this place will be delicious. It's received many reviews.

Su-yeong: Hello. This is a Chinese restaurant, right?

Hyeon-ju: Hey! What are you doing?

Su-yeong: Can I have one black bean noodle and a small sweet and sour pork? What will you have?

Hyeon-ju: Hey, what the... I'll have fried rice, then.

Su-yeong: Add a fried rice to that too. How long will it take? Thirty minutes? Please bring them quickly. And please give us some spicy soup too. I'll pay with a card.

Hyeon-ju: Hey, I wanted to have spicy tteokbokki...

Vocabulary

배고프다	to be hungry
시켜 먹다	to order food for delivery and eat it
귀찮다	to feel bothered, to get tired of
중국집	Chinese restaurant
배달시키다	to order delivery
찾아보다	to look for
종류	kind, type
많다	to be a lot
분식	instant food that is flour-based (such as noodles)
아직	yet, still
시대	generation
뒤떨어지다	to fall behind, to lag behind
쌓여 있다	to be piled up
전단지	flyer (advertisement/menu)
고르다	to pick, to choose
깔다	to install
대충	roughly, without putting in much effort
맵다	to be spicy
맨날	every day
늦다	to be late
엄청나게	tremendously, very
길어지다	to become long
(리뷰가) 달리다	to post (a comment/review)
작다	to be small
추가하다	to add
(시간) 걸리다	to take (time)
갖다 주다	to bring
국물	soup
결제하다	to pay, to make a transaction

Pattern Practice

Study these three grammar patterns that were used in the dialogue and practice!

Pattern I.

아직 NOUN + -도 몰라? casual

You don't even know NOUN yet?

Sentence Used in the Dialogue

너 아직 이런 앱도 몰라?

You don't know about these apps yet?

Sample Sentences

아직 그것도 몰라?

You don't even know that yet?

아직 그 사람도 몰라?

You don't even know that person yet?

Exercises

1. You don't even know that the book was published yet? (the book = 그 책, to be published = 나오다)

   ······›

2. You don't even know the movie yet? (the movie = 그 영화)

   ······›

Answer Key

1. 아직 그 책 나온 것도 몰라? *2.* 아직 그 영화도 몰라?

Applied Patterns

NOUN + -도 몰라?

→ 너 이런 앱도 몰라?

You don't even know about these apps?

아직 NOUN + -도 몰랐어?

→ 너 아직 이런 앱도 몰랐어?

You didn't know about these apps yet?

Pattern 2.

우선 VERB + -아/어/여 봐 casual

First VERB. / First try VERB-ing.

Sentence Used in the Dialogue

우선 종류를 골라 봐.

First choose a category.

Sample Sentences

우선 이거부터 먹어 봐.

First eat this.

우선 이것 좀 봐 봐.

First look at this.

Exercises

1. First talk to Minkyung. (to talk to Minkyung = 민경이한테 얘기하다)

   ......〉

2. First book the tickets. (to book = 예매하다, the tickets = 티켓)

   ......〉

Answer Key

1. 우선 민경이한테 얘기해 봐. *2.* 우선 티켓(을) 예매해 봐.

Applied Patterns

먼저 VERB + -아/어/여 봐

→ 먼저 종류를 골라 봐.
First choose a category.

우선 VERB + -아/어/여

→ 우선 종류를 골라.
First choose a category.

*우선 and 먼저 mean the same thing in this context.

Pattern 3.

대충 VERB + -아/어/여 casual

Just VERB. / Don't think about it too much and just VERB.

Sentence Used in the Dialogue

대충 골라.

Just pick whatever.

Sample Sentences

대충 끝내.

Just finish it.

대충 써.

Just write it.

Exercises

1. Just read it.

……›

2. Just do it.

……›

Answer Key

1. 대충 읽어. *2.* 대충 해.

Applied Patterns

그냥 대충 VERB + -아/어/여

→ 그냥 대충 골라.

Just pick whatever.

*By adding 그냥, you emphasize the meaning of “doing it just for the sake of doing it”.

대충 빨리 VERB + -아/어/여

→ 대충 빨리 골라.

Just quickly pick whatever.

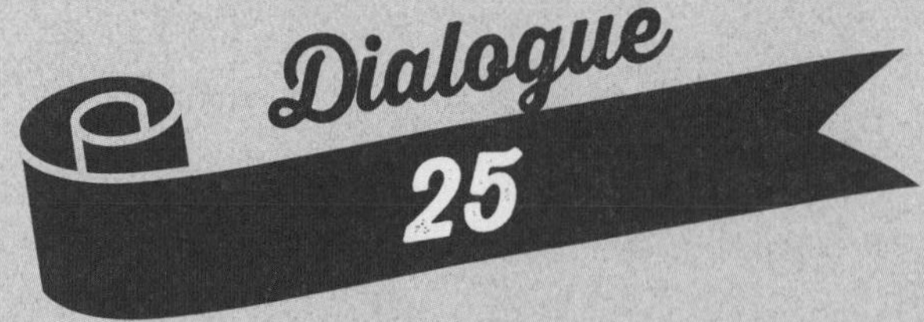

제가 알약을 못 먹어요.

I can't swallow tablets well.

•

Pharmacy

약
VITAMIN C

Dialogue in Korean

약사: 어서 오세요.

민혁: 안녕하세요.

약사: 네, 어떻게 오셨어요?

민혁: 아, 그게... 제가 눈을 깜빡일 때마다 눈 안에 뭐가 걸린 것처럼 아프고 또 점점 붓는 것 같아요.

약사: 아, 그러세요? 제가 좀 볼게요.

민혁: 네. 눈병인가요? 전염되는 건가요? 병원 가야 할까요? 심각한 건 아니죠? 병원 싫은데...

약사: 허허. 눈병 아니고 심각한 것도 아니에요. 다래끼가 나려고 하는 것 같네요.

민혁: 다래끼요? 이거 많이 아픈 건가요?

약사: 더 심해지면 병원 가서 째야 될 수도 있는데 아직 그 정도는 아닌 것 같으니까 일단 약을 챙겨 드세요.

민혁: 째...요?

약사: 네, 더 심해지면요. 손 깨끗이 잘 씻고 눈 절대 비비지 마세요. 약은 하루에 세 번 식후 두 알씩 드시고요.

민혁: 알약...인가요?

약사: 네. 둘 다 알약이에요.

English Translation

Pharmacist: Welcome.

Min-hyeok: Hello.

Pharmacist: Yes, what brought you here?

Min-hyeok: Ah, the thing is... every time I blink, it hurts, like something is stuck in my eyes, and I think they are swelling up.

Pharmacist: Oh, really? Let me take a look.

Min-hyeok: Okay. Is it an eye infection? Is it contagious? Will I have to go see a doctor? It's not serious, right? I don't like hospitals.

Pharmacist: Haha. It's not an eye infection, and it's not serious. I think you're about to get a sty.

Min-hyeok: A sty? Does that hurt a lot?

Pharmacist: If it gets worse, you might have to go to the hospital and get it lanced, but it doesn't seem that bad. So first you should take some medicine regularly.

Min-hyeok: Have it lanced?

Pharmacist: Yeah, if it gets worse. Wash your hands well and don't rub your eyes. Take these pills three times a day after each meal, two pills at a time.

Min-hyeok: Are they tablets?

Pharmacist: Yes, both of them are tablets.

누나: 야, 그냥 먹어! 다 큰 애가 알약을 못 먹어.

약사: 아, 알약을 못 드시나 봐요.

민혁: 네. 제가 알약을 못 먹어요. 예전에 알약 넘기다 목에 걸려서 죽을 뻔 한 적이 있어요.

약사: 아, 그러셨구나...

누나: 삥치지 마! 너 그런 적 없잖아!

민혁: 아, 누나 쫌 조용히 해 봐! 선생님, 혹시 가루약이나 물약은 없나요?

약사: 하하. 알약 못 넘기시는 분들 많아요. 그럼 이 약들은 캡슐 형태니까 이렇게 캡슐을 둘로 분리하면 안에서 가루약이 나와요. 물에 타 드시면 돼요.

민혁: 아, 그래요? 다행이다. 감사합니다! 얼마죠?

약사: 6,500원입니다. 더 필요한 건 없으시고요?

민혁: 네, 없어요.

Older sister: Hey, just take it. You're a big boy and can't even take pills?

Pharmacist: Oh, I suppose you can't swallow tablets easily.

Min-hyeok: Yeah, I can't swallow tablets well. Once, I was trying to swallow some pills and almost died because the pills got stuck in my throat.

Pharmacist: Oh, I see...

Older sister: Don't lie! That never happened to you!

Min-hyeok: Come on. Be quiet, sis. Ma'am, do you have any powdered medicine or liquid medicine by any chance?

Pharmacist: Haha. There are many people who can't swallow pills. Then, since these pills are capsules, if you break the capsules into two like this, the powder that is inside will come out. You can mix that with water and drink it.

Min-hyeok: Oh, really? That's a relief. Thank you! How much is it?

Pharmacist: 6,500 won. Anything else you need?

Min-hyeok: No, nothing else.

Vocabulary

깜빡이다	to blink	깨끗이	clean, neatly
걸리다	to be stuck	씻다	to wash
점점	more and more, gradually, increasingly	비비다	to rub
붓다	to swell up, to become swollen	식후	after meal
눈병	eye infection	알약	pill
전염되다	to be infected, to be infectious	넘기다	to be over, to pass, to swallow
병원	hospital	목에 걸리다	to get stuck in one's throat
심각하다	to be serious	죽다	to die
다래끼	sty	뻥치다	to tell a lie
다래끼가 나다	to have a sty	조용히	quietly
아프다	to hurt, to ache, to be painful	가루약	powdered medicine
심해지다	to become serious	물약	liquid medicine
째다	to cut, to rip	형태	form, shape, style
약	medicine	분리하다	to divide, to isolate
챙겨 먹다	to eat without missing a meal	타 드시다	to mix something with water and drink (honorific)

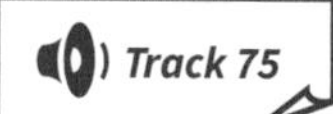

Pattern Practice

Study these three grammar patterns that were used in the dialogue and practice!

Pattern I.

VERB + -아/어/여야 할까요? formal

Will I/we have to VERB? / Do you think I/we should VERB?

Sentence Used in the Dialogue

병원 가야 할까요?

Will I have to go see a doctor?

Sample Sentences

그 사람한테 말해야 할까요?

Do you think I should talk to him?

거기까지 걸어 가야 할까요?

Will I have to walk there?

Exercises

1. Will we have to do it together? (to do = 하다, together = 같이)

  ......〉

2. Do you think I should continue practicing? (to keep practicing = 계속 연습하다)

  ......〉

Answer Key

1. 같이 해야 할까요? *2.* 계속 연습해야 할까요?

Applied Patterns

VERB + -아/어/여 해요?

→ 병원 가야 해요?

Should I go see a doctor?

VERB + -아/어/여야 하나요?

→ 병원 가야 하나요?

Should I go see a doctor?

Pattern 2.

VERB + -(으)려고 하는 것 같네요 formal

I think (someone/something) is about to VERB.

Sentence Used in the Dialogue

다래끼가 나려고 하는 것 같네요.

I think you're about to get a sty.

Sample Sentences

저 아이가 밖으로 나가려고 하는 것 같네요.

I think that kid is about to go outside.

강아지가 먹으려고 하는 것 같아요.

I think the dog is about to eat.

Exercises

1. I think they're about to go to a meeting. (to go to a meeting = 미팅에 가다)

   ······〉

2. I think she is about to pick up the phone. (to pick up the phone = 전화를 받다)

   ······〉

Answer Key

1. 미팅에 가려고 하는 것 같네요. *2.* 전화를 받으려고 하는 것 같네요.

Applied Patterns

VERB + -(으)려고 하는 것 같아요

→ 다래끼가 나려고 하는 것 같아요.
I think you're about to get a sty.

*같아요 is a more neutral and plain way to say "I think" than 같네요, which emphasizes the fact that you are making an observation.

VERB + -(으)려고 하네요

→ 다래끼가 나려고 하네요.
I think you're about to get a sty.

*You can also simply say -(으)려고 하네요 by removing the -것 같다 part.

Pattern 3.

VERB + -(으)ㄹ 뻔한 적이 있어요 formal

I almost PAST TENSE VERB once.

Sentence Used in the Dialogue

죽을 뻔한 적이 있어요.

I almost died once.

Sample Sentences

물에 빠져서 못 나올 뻔한 적이 있어요.

I almost couldn't get out of the water after I fell in once.

절벽에서 떨어질 뻔한 적이 있어요.

I almost fell down from a cliff.

Exercises

1. I almost lost a friend of mine. (to lose = 잃다, a friend of mine = 친구)

……〉

2. I almost couldn't come back once. (couldn't come back = 못 돌아오다)

……〉

Answer Key

1. 친구를 잃을 뻔한 적이 있어요. *2.* 못 돌아올 뻔한 적이 있어요.

Applied Patterns

VERB + -(으)ㄹ 뻔했어요

→ 죽을 뻔했어요.

I almost died once.

*Instead of using -(으)ㄹ 뻔하다 and -(으)ㄴ 적이 있다 together, you can simply say -(으)ㄹ 뻔하다 in the past tense to mean the same thing.

VERB + -(으)ㄹ 뻔한 적이 있었어요

→ 죽을 뻔한 적이 있었어요.

I almost died once.

*Even though the sentence talks about something in the past, you can make the meaning more clear by changing 있어요 to 있었어요.

주사 놓을게요.

I'll give you a shot.

Hospital

Dialogue in Korean

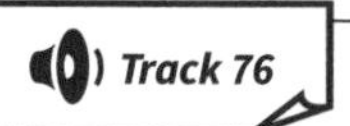

간호사: 안녕하세요. 어디가 안 좋으세요?

수민: 아, 감기 몸살이 심하게 걸려서요.

간호사: 네, 이거 작성해 주시고 잠시만 앉아서 기다려 주세요.

수민: 네. 얼마나 기다려야 하나요?

간호사: 십 분 정도만 기다려 주세요.

수민: 네.

간호사: 김수민 씨, 들어오세요.

수민: 네.

의사: 안녕하세요.

수민: 네, 안녕하세요.

의사: 감기 걸리셨어요?

수민: 네. 추운 날씨에 계속 밖에서 활동했더니 감기에 제대로 걸린 것 같아요.

의사: 증상이 어떠세요?

수민: 목이 너무 따갑고 아프고요. 기운이 하나도 없어요.

의사: 아이고. 요즘 유행하는 독감에 걸리신 것 같네요. 자 그럼 한번 볼게요. 입 '아' 하고 벌려 보세요.

English Translation

Nurse: Hello. What is bothering you?

Su-min: Oh, I have a severe cold and my body aches.

Nurse: Okay. Please fill this in, and sit and wait for just a little bit.

Su-min: Okay. How long should I wait?

Nurse: Please wait about ten minutes or so.

Su-min: Okay.

Nurse: Sumin Kim, please come in.

Su-min: Yes.

Doctor: Hello.

Su-min: Yes, hi.

Doctor: Have you caught a cold?

Su-min: Yes, I stayed outside in the cold weather, so I think I've come down with a bad cold.

Doctor: What are your symptoms?

Su-min: My throat is really sore and painful. I have no energy.

Doctor: Oh... It looks like you've come down with the flu, which is going around these days. Well, let's take a look. Open your mouth and say "Ah".

수민: 아...

의사: 편도선이 심하게 부었네요. 열 좀 잴게요. 귀 좀 보여 주세요.

수민: 네.

의사: 열도 많이 나네요.

수민: 네, 선생님. 주사 좀 놔 주세요.

의사: 네. 주사 한 대 놔 드릴게요. 주사 맞으면 좀 괜찮아질 거예요.

수민: 네, 감사합니다.

의사: 여기 누워서 바지 살짝 내리고 계세요. 간호사 선생님 금방 오실 거예요.

수민: 네? 선생님이 주사 놔 주시는 거 아닌가요?

의사: 주사는 간호사 선생님이 놔 주실 거예요.

수민: 아... 네...

간호사: 주사 놓을게요. 바지 내려 주세요. 더 내리셔야 돼요.

수민: 아... 네...

간호사: 네. 다 됐습니다.

Su-min: Ah...

Doctor: Your tonsils are severely swollen. Let me take your temperature. Please show me your ear.

Su-min: Yes.

Doctor: You have a high fever too.

Su-min: Yes, sir. Please give me some medicine.

Doctor: Okay. I'll give you a shot in your rear. You will feel a little better after getting a shot.

Su-min: Okay, thank you.

Doctor: Please lie down here and lower your pants a little bit. The nurse will be here soon.

Su-min: Huh? You're not giving me the shot?

Doctor: The shot will be given to you by the nurse.

Su-min: Oh, I see...

Nurse: I'll give you the shot. Please lower your pants. You need to lower them a little more.

Su-min: Oh, I see...

Nurse: Alright. It's done.

Vocabulary

감기	cold
몸살	body ache
심하다	to be serious
걸리다	to get (sick), to catch a disease
작성하다	to fill out
잠시만	for a little bit, for just a little while
계속	continuously, consecutively
활동하다	to work, to act
제대로	properly, right
증상	symptom
목	throat
따갑다	to be sore
기운이 없다	to have no energy, to feel down
유행하다	to be popular, to be in fashion
독감	flu
벌리다	to open
편도선	tonsil
붓다	to swell up, to become swollen
열	fever
재다	to measure
보여 주다	to show
주사	injection, shot
주사를 놓다	to measure
괜찮다	to be okay, to be alright
눕다	to lie down
살짝	slightly
내리다	to lower, to take down
간호사	nurse

Pattern Practice

Study these three grammar patterns that were used in the dialogue and practice!

Pattern I.

VERB + -았/었/였더니

I PAST TENSE VERB and as a result...

Sentence Used in the Dialogue

밖에서 활동했더니 감기에 제대로 걸린 것 같아요.

I stayed outside for a long time and I think I've come down with a bad cold.

Sample Sentences

너무 오래 달렸더니 어지러워요.

I ran for a long time and now I'm dizzy.

오늘 아침에 일찍 일어났더니 너무 졸려요.

I woke up early this morning and as a result I am so sleepy.

Exercises

1. I ate too much and now my stomach hurts. (to have a stomachache = 배 아프다, to eat too much = 너무 많이 먹다)

   ......〉

2. I stayed home for a long time and as a result I'm bored. (to feel bored = 심심하다, to stay home = 집에 있다, too long = 오래)

······〉

Answer Key

1. 너무 많이 먹었더니 배 아파요. *2.* 집에 오래 있었더니 심심해요. or 오래 집에 있었더니 심심해요.

Applied Patterns

VERB + -아/어/여서

→ 밖에서 활동해서 감기에 제대로 걸린 것 같아요.
I stayed outside for a long time and I think I've come down with a bad cold.

VERB + -고 나니까

→ 밖에서 활동하고 나니까 감기에 제대로 걸린 것 같아요
After staying outside for a long time, I think I've come down with a bad cold.

Pattern 2.

VERB + -(으)면 VERB + -(으)ㄹ 거예요 formal

After..., you will VERB. / If..., you will VERB.

Sentence Used in the Dialogue

주사 맞으면 좀 괜찮아질 거예요.

After getting a shot, you will feel a little better.

Sample Sentences

그 사람 만나면 그 사람이 얘기해 줄 거예요.

If you meet that person, he will tell you.

시간이 지나면 알게 될 거예요.

After some time passes, you will know.

Exercises

1. After you have taken some medicine, you will get better. (to have some medicine = 약 먹다, to get better = 낫다)

   ......〉

2. If he comes back next month, we will meet again. (to come back = 돌아오다, next month = 다음 달)

   ......〉

Answer Key

1. 약 먹으면 나을 거예요. *2.* 다음 달에 그 사람이 돌아오면 다시 만날 거예요 or 그 사람이 다음 달에 돌아오면 다시 만날 거예요.

Applied Patterns

VERB + -(으)면 VERB + -(으)ㄹ 수도 있어요

→ 주사 맞으면 좀 괜찮아질 수도 있어요.

If you get a shot, you might feel better.

VERB + -(으)면 VERB + -아/어/여요

→ 주사 맞으면 좀 괜찮아져요.

If you get a shot, you will get better.

Pattern 3.

더 VERB + -아/어/여야 돼요 formal

You need to VERB more.

Sentence Used in the Dialogue

더 내리셔야 돼요.

You need to lower them a little more.

Sample Sentences

더 가야 돼요.

You need to go further.

더 기다려야 돼요.

You need to wait more.

Exercises

1. It needs to be brighter. (to be brighter = 더 밝다)

······〉

2. You need to eat more. (to eat more = 더 먹다)

⋯⋯〉

Answer Key

1. 더 밝아야 돼요. *2.* 더 먹어야 돼요.

Applied Patterns

더 VERB + -아/어/여야 해요

→ 더 내리셔야 해요.

You need to lower them a little more.

*-야 해요 and -야 돼요 mean the same thing.

더 VERB + -아/어/여야 돼 casual

→ 더 내려야 돼.

You need to lower them a little more.

*Removing -요 at the end makes the sentence more casual.

그냥 몸이 좀 안 좋네.

I just don’t feel well.

•

Not Feeling Well

$x^n + y^n$
D
C
B
A
E

Dialogue in Korean

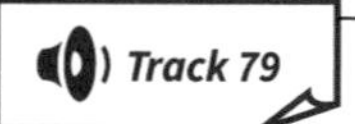

다영: 다희야, 왜 그래? 어디 아파? 안색이 안 좋은데?

다희: 응? 어... 그냥 몸이 좀 안 좋네.

다영: 왜? 감기 걸렸어? 아님 뭐 잘못 먹었어?

다희: 아니. 뭐 잘못 먹은 건 아니고. 어제부터 기운이 없고 몸이 으슬으슬 떨리더니 계속 더 심해지네.

다영: 감기네 감기. 몸살감기 걸렸나 보다.

다희: 응. 그런 것 같아.

다영: 요즘 독감이 유행이더라. 세경이도 감기 걸렸다고 오늘 학교 안 왔어.

다희: 아, 그래?

다영: 응. 심하게 걸렸나 봐. 오늘 새벽부터 응급실 갔다 왔다더라.

다희: 정말?

다영: 응. 너는 약은 먹었어?

다희: 응, 약 먹었어.

다영: 너도 병원 가 봐야 되는 거 아냐?

다희: 아냐. 그 정돈 아니야. 다음 주 시험이라서 오늘 수업 빠지면 안 돼.

English Translation

Da-yeong: Da-hee. What's wrong? Are you sick? You don't look well.

Da-hee: Huh? Yeah... I just don't feel well.

Da-yeong: Why? Have you caught a cold? Or did you eat something bad?

Da-hee: No, I didn't eat anything bad. I haven't had any energy since yesterday. I started feeling chilly, and it's getting worse and worse.

Da-yeong: It's a cold. I think you caught a cold and now your body aches.

Da-hee: Yeah, I think so.

Da-yeong: I heard that the flu is going around these days. Se-gyeong also didn't come to school today because she caught a cold.

Da-hee: Oh, really?

Da-yeong: Yeah, I guess she caught a really bad one. I heard that she went to the emergency room early in the morning today.

Da-hee: Really?

Da-yeong: Yeah. Did you take some medicine?

Da-hee: Yeah, I took some medicine.

Da-yeong: Shouldn't you go see a doctor too?

Da-hee: No, it's not that bad. The exam is next week, so I can't skip classes today.

다영: 으이구. 내가 필기해서 보여 줄게. 양호실이라도 가서 좀 쉬고 와.

다희: 아냐, 괜찮아. 말이라도 고맙다.

다영: 그래, 그럼. 몸 더 안 좋아지면 꼭 병원 가 봐.

다희: 알겠어. 고마워.

다영: 응.

선생님: 김다희. 너 왜 그래? 어디 아파?

다희: 아... 괜찮아요.

선생님: 괜찮기는. 너 머리가 불덩이야. 금방 쓰러질 것 같아.

다희: 아... 저 감기에 좀 걸려서... 선생님, 저 양호실에 좀 갔다 올게요.

선생님: 그래, 얼른 다녀와. 양호 선생님이 조퇴하라고 하시면 바로 조퇴하고 병원 가.

다희: 네. 알겠습니다. 다녀올게요.

Da-yeong: Come on. I will take some notes and show them to you. At least go to the nurse's room and get some rest.

Da-hee: No, I'm good. Thanks for the offer though.

Da-yeong: Okay, then. If you feel worse, make sure you go to the hospital.

Da-hee: I got it. Thank you.

Da-yeong: Okay.

Teacher: Da-hee, what's wrong? Are you sick?

Da-hee: Ah... I'm alright.

Teacher: You're not alright. Your head is on fire. It looks like you're about to faint.

Da-hee: Ah... I caught a cold... Let me go visit the nurse's office.

Teacher: Okay. Hurry up. If the nurse tells you to leave early, take the rest of the day off and go to the hospital quickly.

Da-hee: Okay. I understand. See you.

Vocabulary

Track 80

안색이 안 좋다	to not look well
몸이 안 좋다	to not feel well
걸리다	to get (sick), to catch a disease
으슬으슬	feeling chilly
떨리다	to tremble
계속	continuously, consecutively
심해지다	to get worse
유행	fashion, trend
오늘	today
심하게	severely, terribly
새벽	dawn
응급실	emergency room
약	medicine
병원	hospital
정도	level, degree, approximately
시험	test, exam
수업	class
빠지다	to be omitted, to not be included
필기하다	to take notes
보여 주다	to show
양호실	nurse's office
쉬다	to rest
괜찮다	to be okay, to be alright
고맙다	to be thankful, to be grateful
머리	head
불덩이	fireball
쓰러지다	to faint
조퇴하다	to leave school/office early

Pattern Practice

Study these three grammar patterns that were used in the dialogue and practice!

Pattern I.

계속 더 ADJECTIVE + -아/어/여지네 casual

(SUBJECT) am/is/are getting more and more ADJECTIVE.

Sentence Used in the Dialogue

계속 더 심해지네.

It's getting worse and worse.

Sample Sentences

계속 더 멀어지네.

It's getting farther and farther.

계속 더 배고파지네.

I'm getting hungrier and hungrier.

Exercises

1. I'm getting more and more curious. (to be curious = 궁금하다)

    ......〉

2. It's getting bigger and bigger. (to be bigger = 더 크다)

    ......〉

Answer Key

1. 계속 더 궁금해지네. *2.* 계속 더 커지네.

Applied Patterns

계속 ADJECTIVE + -아/어/여지네

→ 계속 심해지네.

It's getting worse and worse.

*Even without the word 더, which means "more", the sentence will have the same meaning here.

계속 더 ADJECTIVE + -아/어/여져

→ 계속 더 심해져.

It's getting worse and worse.

*-져 is a more neutral ending than -지네, which shows one's observation.

Pattern 2.

VERB + -(으)면 안 돼 casual

I can't VERB. / I shouldn't VERB.

Sentence Used in the Dialogue

오늘 수업 빠지면 안 돼.

I can't skip classes today.

Sample Sentences

나 이거 다 먹으면 안 돼.

I can't eat them all.

나 오늘 놀면 안 돼.

I shouldn't just play today.

Exercises

1. I can't get drunk today. (to get drunk = 취하다, today = 오늘)

   ……>

2. I shouldn't exercise today. (to exercise = 운동하다, today = 오늘)

   ……>

Answer Key

1. 나 오늘 취하면 안 돼.. *2.* 나 오늘 운동하면 안 돼.

Applied Patterns

VERB + -(으)면 안 돼요 formal

→ 오늘 수업 빠지면 안 돼요.

I can't skip classes today.

Pattern 3.

금방 VERB + -(으)ㄹ 것 같아 casual

It looks like (SUBJECT) is about to VERB.

Sentence Used in the Dialogue

금방 쓰러질 것 같아.

It looks like you're about to faint.

Sample Sentences

금방 시작할 것 같아.

It looks like it's about to start.

금방 도착할 것 같아.

It looks like he's about to arrive.

Exercises

1. It looks like we're about to get a call. (to get a call = 전화 오다)

    ......〉

2. It looks like they're about to depart. (to depart = 출발하다)

    ......〉

Answer Key

1. 금방 전화 올 것 같아. *2.* 금방 출발할 것 같아.

Applied Patterns

막 VERB + -(으)ㄹ 것 같아

→ 막 쓰러질 것 같아.

It looks like you're about to faint.

*Even though 막 can mean many things, in this context it means "soon" or "anytime now".

곧 VERB + -(으)ㄹ 것 같아

→ 곧 쓰러질 것 같아.

It looks like you will faint soon.

어디로 모실까요?

Where to?

•

Taxi

택시
택시

Dialogue in Korean

택시 기사: 어서 오세요.

경호: 안녕하세요.

택시 기사: 어디로 모실까요?

경호: 구로 시장으로 가 주세요.

택시 기사: 네.

경호: 기사님, 얼마쯤 나올까요?

택시 기사: 지금은 막히는 시간대가 아니니까 15,000원 정도 나올 것 같네요. 여기서 성산대교 타실 거예요? 아니면 좌측으로 돌아서 갈까요?

경호: 성산대교로 가 주세요.

택시 기사: 네. 댁이 거기이신가 봐요.

경호: 네. 구로 시장 근처에 집이 있어요.

택시 기사: 거기는 집값이 비싸지 않아요?

경호: 주위 다른 곳에 비해서 좀 싼 편이에요. 그리고 교통편도 좋아서 살기 좋은 것 같아요.

택시 기사: 시장 근처에서 살면 좀 시끄럽고 그렇지 않나요?

경호: 생각보다 그렇게 시끄럽지는 않더라고요. 그리고 아침 일찍 출근하고 저녁 늦게 집에 들어오니까 주위가 그렇게 시끄러운지 모르겠더라고요.

English Translation

Taxi Driver: Welcome.

Kyeong-ho: Hi.

Taxi Driver: Where to?

Kyeong-ho: Please take me to Guro Market.

Taxi Driver: Okay.

Kyeong-ho: About how much will it be?

Taxi Driver: I think it will be around 15,000 won since it's not rush hour now. Do you want to take Seong-san Bridge from here? Or shall we turn left?

Kyeong-ho: Please go to Seong-san Bridge.

Taxi Driver: Okay. I guess your house is around there.

Kyeong-ho: Yes, my house is near Guro Market.

Taxi Driver: Are house prices not that high around there?

Kyeong-ho: It's a bit cheaper compared to other places nearby. And transportation is convenient, so I think it's a good place to live.

Taxi Driver: If you live near a market, isn't it a bit noisy?

Kyeong-ho: I find that it's not that noisy, unlike what you would think. And since I go to work early and come home late in the evening, I don't really realize if the neighborhood is that noisy.

택시 기사: 구로 시장이 꽤 크죠?

경호: 네. 엄청 커요. 최근에 리모델링을 했는데 깔끔하게 잘 해 놨더라고요.

택시 기사: 장 보러 가실 때 많이 편하시겠어요.

경호: 그렇죠. 시장이 바로 코앞이니까. 요금은 현금으로 드리는 게 나아요? 아니면 카드로 내는 게 나아요?

택시 기사: 현금이든 카드든 상관없어요. 손님이 편하신 대로 내 주시면 돼요.

경호: 그렇군요. 어떤 기사님은 현금으로 내면 거스름돈 주기 번거롭다고 카드를 선호하시더라고요.

택시 기사: 네. 그런 분도 계시죠. 이제 거의 다 왔네요. 어디에 세워 드릴까요?

경호: 조금 더 가셔서요. 저기 빵집 앞에서 세워 주세요.

택시 기사: 네. 도착했습니다.

경호: 감사합니다. 안녕히 가세요.

택시 기사: 네. 안녕히 가세요.

Taxi Driver: Guro Market is pretty big, right?

Kyeong-ho: Yes, it's really big. They remodeled it recently, and made it really nice and neat.

Taxi Driver: It must be very convenient when you go grocery shopping.

Kyeong-ho: That's right. Because the market is right around the corner. Is it better for me to pay the fare in cash or with a card?

Taxi Driver: Cash or card, it doesn't matter. Just pay with whatever is convenient for you.

Kyeong-ho: I see. Some drivers prefer card saying that if I pay in cash, it's a lot of hassle to give me small change.

Taxi Driver: Yes, there are some people like that. We are almost there now. Where shall I drop you off?

Kyeong-ho: Please go straight just a little bit more, and pull over in front of the bakery over there.

Taxi Driver: Okay. We have arrived.

Kyeong-ho: Thank you. Bye.

Taxi Driver: Okay. Bye.

Vocabulary

모시다	to take to (honorific)
얼마쯤	about how much
(차가) 막히다	traffic is bad, congested
타다	to ride
좌측	left side
돌아서 가다	to take a detour, to turn around and go
댁	someone's house, someone's place (honorific)
집값	house price
비싸다	to be expensive
주위	surroundings
다른 곳	somewhere else, another place
비하다	to compare, to be compared
싸다	to be cheap
교통편	transportation
시끄럽다	to be loud, to be noisy
생각	thought
깔끔하다	to be neat
장 보러 가다	to go grocery shopping
편하다	to be comfortable
코앞	right around the corner, happening very soon
요금	charge, fee, fare
현금	cash
드리다	to give (honorific)
낫다	to be better
상관없다	to not matter
거스름돈	small change
번거롭다	to be cumbersome, to be inconvenient
선호하다	to prefer
다 오다	to arrive
세워 드리다	to drop someone off (honorific), to stop the car for someone (honorific)

Pattern Practice

Study these three grammar patterns that were used in the dialogue and practice!

Pattern I.

NOUN + -에 비해서 ADJECTIVE + -(으)ㄴ 편이에요 formal

(SUBJECT) am/is/are relatively ADJECTIVE compared to NOUN.

Sentence Used in the Dialogue

주위 다른 곳에 비해서 좀 싼 편이에요.

It's a bit cheaper compared to other places nearby.

Sample Sentences

저는 제 친구들에 비해서 내성적인 편이에요.

I am relatively introverted compared to my friends.

다른 휴대폰에 비해서 성능이 좋은 편이에요.

It has relatively higher specs compared to other phones.

Exercises

1. The food here is relatively better compared to that of other places. (to be good = 맛있다, other places = 다른 곳들)

   ......>

2. It's relatively hotter here compared to other countries. (to be hot = 덥다, other countries = 다른 나라들)

   ......>

Answer Key

1. 다른 곳들에 비해서 맛있는 편이에요. 2. 다른 나라들에 비해서 더운 편이에요.

Applied Patterns

NOUN + -에 비해서 ADJECTIVE + -아/어/여요

→ 주위 다른 곳에 비해서 좀 싸요.

It's a bit cheaper compared to other places nearby.

*-(으)ㄴ 편이에요 means "it's kind of" or "it tends to be", so by not saying 편이에요, you make the statement more clear.

NOUN + -에 비해 ADJECTIVE + -(으)ㄴ 편이에요

→ 주위 다른 곳에 비해 좀 싼 편이에요.

It's a bit cheaper compared to other places nearby.

*-에 비해서 and -에 비해 mean exactly the same thing.

Pattern 2.

생각보다 ADJECTIVE + -더라고요 formal

I found that it was more ADJECTIVE than I had thought.

Sentence Used in the Dialogue

생각보다 그렇게 시끄럽지는 않더라고요.

I find that it's not that noisy, unlike what you would think.

Sample Sentences

생각보다 비싸더라고요.

I found that it was more expensive than I had thought it would be.

생각보다 잘하더라고요.

I found that he was better than I had thought.

Exercises

1. I found that it was farther than I had thought. (to be far = 멀다)

 ......〉

2. I found that it was harder than I had thought. (to be hard = 어렵다)

 ......〉

Answer Key

1. 생각보다 멀더라고요. *2.* 생각보다 어렵더라고요.

Applied Patterns

생각보다 ADJECTIVE + -았/었/였어요

→ 생각보다 그렇게 시끄럽지는 않았어요.

I found that it wasn't as noisy as I had thought.

*-더라고(요) is a way to show one's past observation, however you can convey a similar meaning for this sentence without it.

생각보다 ADJECTIVE + -던데요

→ 생각보다 그렇게 시끄럽지는 않던데요.

I found that it wasn't as noisy as I had thought.

*-던데요 has the same purpose as -더라고요, but when you say -던데요, you usually expect the listener's response.

Pattern 3.

NOUN + -(이)든 NOUN + -(이)든 상관없어요 formal

NOUN or NOUN, it doesn't matter.

Sentence Used in the Dialogue

현금이든 카드든 상관없어요.

Cash or card, it doesn't matter.

Sample Sentences

크리스든 제임스든 상관없어요.

Chris or James, it doesn't matter.

남자든 여자든 상관없어요.

Man or woman, it doesn't matter.

Exercises

1. Bread or snacks, it doesn't matter. (bread = 빵, snacks = 과자)

……〉

2. Red or white, it doesn't matter. (red = 빨간색, white = 하얀색)

······>

Answer Key

1. 빵이든 과자든 상관없어요. *2.* 빨간색이든 하얀색이든 상관없어요.

Applied Patterns

NOUN + -(이)든 NOUN + -(이)든 아무 상관없어요

→ 현금이든 카드든 아무 상관없어요.

Cash or card, it doesn't matter.

*아무 means "at all" or "any", so it emphasizes the fact that it doesn't matter.

NOUN + -(이)든 NOUN + -(이)든 둘 다 괜찮아요

→ 현금이든 카드든 둘 다 괜찮아요.

Cash or card, both are okay.

저기, 지하철 표 사려면 어떻게 해야 되죠?

Excuse me, what should I do to buy subway tickets?

•

Subway

Dialogue in Korean

영민: 저기, 지하철 표 사려면 어떻게 해야 되죠?

역무원: 아, 요즘은 저기 저 기계로 다 해요.

영민: 아, 제가 지하철을 처음 타 봐서...

역무원: 같이 가시죠. 제가 도와 드릴게요. 자, 여기 도착역을 선택하고 돈을 넣으면 이렇게 일회용 카드가 나와요.

영민: 아, 감사합니다!

역무원: 보증금 500원 포함돼 있으니까 도착해서 꼭 보증금 환급기에 카드 넣고 보증금 찾아가세요.

영민: 네, 알겠습니다. 감사합니다.

영민: 저기 죄송한데, 이거 합정역 가는 거 맞나요?

행인: 합정역이요? 어... 아닐 텐데... 잠시만요. 아, 이 방향이 아니네요! 반대 방향으로 가셔야 돼요.

영민: 아, 그래요?

행인: 네, 이쪽으로 올라가셔서 반대쪽으로 다시 내려가서 타세요.

영민: 네, 감사합니다.

English Translation

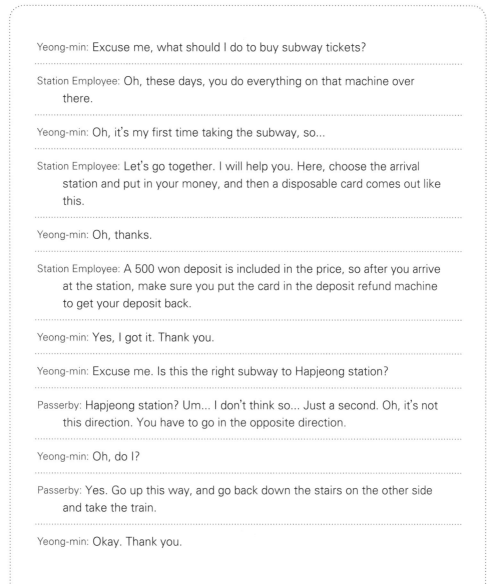

Yeong-min: Excuse me, what should I do to buy subway tickets?

Station Employee: Oh, these days, you do everything on that machine over there.

Yeong-min: Oh, it's my first time taking the subway, so...

Station Employee: Let's go together. I will help you. Here, choose the arrival station and put in your money, and then a disposable card comes out like this.

Yeong-min: Oh, thanks.

Station Employee: A 500 won deposit is included in the price, so after you arrive at the station, make sure you put the card in the deposit refund machine to get your deposit back.

Yeong-min: Yes, I got it. Thank you.

Yeong-min: Excuse me. Is this the right subway to Hapjeong station?

Passerby: Hapjeong station? Um... I don't think so... Just a second. Oh, it's not this direction. You have to go in the opposite direction.

Yeong-min: Oh, do I?

Passerby: Yes. Go up this way, and go back down the stairs on the other side and take the train.

Yeong-min: Okay. Thank you.

(통화 중)

영민: 응. 나 이제 지하철 타!

수민: 뭐? 이제 탄다고? 왜 이렇게 늦었어?

영민: 좀 헤맸어. 나 지하철 처음 타 보잖아.

수민: 뭐? 지하철을 처음 타 본다고?

영민: 그래. 나 사는 동네는 지하철이 없어.

수민: 헐. 너 별에서 왔니?

영민: 그래. 별에서 왔다! 쫌만 기다려. 금방 가!

수민: 알겠어. 지하철에서 길 잃지 말고 조심히 와.

(On the phone)

Yeong-min: Yes, I'm taking the subway now.

Su-min: What? You're taking it now? What made you so late?

Yeong-min: I got a little lost. You know it's my first time taking the subway.

Su-min: What? It's your first time taking the subway?

Yeong-min: Yeah. Where I live, there is no subway.

Su-min: Oh my god. Are you from a star?

Yeong-min: Yes, I'm from a star. Just wait a little bit. I'll be there soon.

Su-min: Okay. Come here safely and don't get lost in the subway.

Vocabulary

저기	there	환급기	refund machine
지하철	subway	찾아가다	to pick up, to get something back
표	ticket	죄송하다	to be sorry
요즘	these days	방향	direction
기계	machine	반대	opposite
타다	to ride	올라가다	to go up
도와 드리다	to help (honorific)	반대쪽	opposite side
도착역	arrival station	내려가다	to go down
선택하다	to choose	늦다	to be late
넣다	to put something in, to add	헤매다	to get lost and wander around
일회용	disposable	살다	to live
카드	card	동네	neighborhood, area
보증금	deposit	별	star
포함되다	to be included	길 잃다	to get lost
도착하다	to arrive	조심히	carefully

Pattern Practice

Study these three grammar patterns that were used in the dialogue and practice!

Pattern I.

VERB + -(으)려면 어떻게 해야 되죠? formal

What should I do to VERB?

Sentence Used in the Dialogue

지하철 표 사려면 어떻게 해야 되죠?

What should I do to buy subway tickets?

Sample Sentences

여기 통과하려면 어떻게 해야 되죠?

What should I do to pass through here?

시험에 합격하려면 어떻게 해야 되죠?

What should I do to pass the exam?

Exercises

1. What should I do to go there? (to go = 가다, there = 저기로)

   ······〉

2. What should I do to turn off the computer? (to turn off = 끄다, computer = 컴퓨터)

   ······〉

Answer Key

1. 저기로 가려면 어떻게 해야 되죠? *2.* 컴퓨터 끄려면 어떻게 해야 되죠?

Applied Patterns

VERB + -(으)려면 어떻게 해야 하죠?

→ 지하철 표 사려면 어떻게 해야 하죠?
What should I do to buy subway tickets?

*해야 하다 and 해야 되다 mean the same thing.

VERB + -(으)려면 어떻게 해야 돼? casual

→ 지하철 표 사려면 어떻게 해야 돼?
What should I do to buy subway tickets?

Pattern 2.

이거 VERB + -는 거 맞나요? formal

Is this the right NOUN to VERB? / Is this supposed to VERB?

Sentence Used in the Dialogue

이거 합정역 가는 거 맞나요?

Is this the right subway to Hapjeong station?

Sample Sentences

이거 명동 가는 거 맞나요?

Is this the right bus/subway to Myeong-dong?

이거 이렇게 작동하는 거 맞나요?

Is this supposed to work like this?

Exercises

1. Is this supposed to make this kind of sound? (to make this kind of sound = 이런 소리 나다)

……〉

2. Is this the right train to Busan? (Busan = 부산)

……〉

Answer Key

1. 이거 이런 소리 나는 거 맞나요? *2.* 이거 부산 가는 거 맞나요?

Applied Patterns

이거 VERB + -나요?

→ 이거 합정역 가나요?

Does this go to Hapjeong station?

이거 VERB + -는 건가요?

→ 이거 합정역 가는 건가요?

Does this go to Hapjeong station?

Pattern 3.

VERB + -지 말고 VERB + -아/어/여 casual

Don't VERB and VERB.

Sentence Used in the Dialogue

지하철에서 길 잃지 말고 조심히 와.

Come here safely and don't get lost in the subway.

Sample Sentences

끊지 말고 계속 통화 해.

Don't hang up and keep talking on the phone.

사진 그걸로 찍지 말고 이거로 찍어.

Don't take pictures with that. Do it with this one.

Exercises

1. Don't open the window and just turn on the air conditioner. (to open = 열다, the window = 창문, to turn on the air conditioner = 에어컨 켜다)

   ......〉

2. Don't go there and just come here. (to go there = 거기로 가다, to come here = 여기로 오다)

   ......〉

Answer Key

1. 창문 열지 말고 에어컨 켜. *2.* 거기로 가지 말고 여기로 와.

Applied Patterns

VERB + -지 말고 VERB + -아/어/여야 돼.

→ 지하철에서 길 잃지 말고 조심히 와야 돼요.

You should should come here safely without getting lost in the subway.

VERB + -지 말고 VERB + -(으)세요 formal

→ 지하철에서 길 잃지 말고 조심히 오세요.

Don't get lost in the subway and just come here safely.

저 이번에 비행기 처음 타 보는 거예요.

This is my first time on an airplane.

•

Airplane

Dialogue in Korean

소연: 언니, 저 이번에 비행기 처음 타 보는 거예요.

지혜: 진짜? 고등학교 수학여행 갈 때 비행기 안 탔어?

소연: 네. 저희 수학여행 배 타고 갔었어요.

지혜: 제주도를?

소연: 네.

지혜: 그랬구나. 근데 나 같으면 비행기 타 보고 싶어서라도 제주도나 해외 여행 가려고 했을 것 같은데, 대학 다닐 동안 한 번도 안 갔던 거야?

소연: 네. 저는 여행을 막 그렇게 좋아하진 않아서, 여행 가려고 돈 모았다가도 사고 싶은 게 생기면 그 돈으로 물건을 사 버렸어요. 노트북이나 그런 거요.

지혜: 아, 정말? 여행을 안 좋아하다니! 근데 사실 비행기 막상 타 보면 별거 없어. 좁고.

소연: 그래도 너무 아쉬워요. 탔다가 금방 내릴 테니까. 좀 더 길게 타고 싶은데.

지혜: 다음에 돈 모아서 해외여행 가. 멀리 여행 가는 것도 조금이라도 어릴 때 가야 된대. 나이 먹을수록 장시간 비행기 타면 힘드니까.

소연: 그래요? 저는 좋기만 할 것 같은데.

English Translation

So-yeon: Eonni, this is my first time on an airplane.

Ji-hye: Really? You didn't take an airplane when you went on your high school excursion?

So-yeon: Yeah. We took a boat when we went on our trip.

Ji-hye: To Jeju Island?

So-yeon: Yes.

Ji-hye: I see. If I were you, since you wanted to take an airplane, I would have gone to Jeju Island or on an overseas trip at least. You never went anywhere during your college years?

So-yeon: Yup. I don't really like traveling that much, so even after saving up money, if there was something I wanted to buy, I just bought it with that money. A laptop or things like that.

Ji-hye: Oh, really? You don't like traveling? Actually, when you are in the airplane, there's nothing special. It's really cramped.

So-yeon: But still, it's too bad, because we'll be getting off the airplane soon after we get on it. I want to ride for a little longer.

Ji-hye: Next time, save your money and go on an overseas trip. They say you should go on long-distance trips while you are still young. The older you get, the harder it becomes to fly for an extended period of time.

So-yeon: Really? I think I'll just be happy without it.

지혜: 너도 몇 번만 타 보면 비행기 오래 타는 게 얼마나 곤욕인지 알 수 있을 거야.

소연: 비행기에 액체류 반입 제한 있다던데, 그건 뭐예요?

지혜: 아! 국제선 탈 때 액체류는 100ml 이하 용기에 담긴 것만 가지고 탈 수 있거든. 근데 우리는 국내선이라 상관없어.

소연: 아... 그렇게 많은 액체를 사람들은 왜 가지고 타죠?

지혜: 대부분 화장품이나 치약, 아니면 마실 물, 이런 거지, 뭐. 나도 지난번에 아무 생각 없이 물병 들고 타려다가 버리라고 해서 한 모금밖에 안 마신 거였는데, 버렸잖아.

소연: 아, 치약 이런 것도 액체류에 속하는구나. 몰랐어요.

지혜: 응. 액체류랑 젤류 둘 다 제한한대. 자, 그럼 비행기 타러 들어가 볼까?

소연: 꺅! 신나요. 면세점에서 쇼핑해야지!

지혜: 소연아, 미안하지만 김포공항 국내선에는 면세점이 없단다. 너무 실망하지 마. 제주공항에는 면세점 있으니까 올 때 쇼핑 마음껏 하렴.

Ji-hye: Once you take an airplane a few times, you will know how much of a pain it is to fly for a long time.

So-yeon: I heard that there is a limit to carrying liquid onto the airplane. What is that about?

Ji-hye: Oh, when you take an international flight, you can only board the plane with liquid that's in a container that is less than 100ml. But we are on a domestic flight, so it doesn't affect us.

So-yeon: Oh... Why do people carry so much liquid onboard?

Ji-hye: It's mostly cosmetics, toothpaste, or drinking water, stuff like that, you know. I was about to get on a plane with a water bottle without thinking once, and they told me to throw it away, so I did, even though I had only taken a sip out of it.

So-yeon: Oh, things like toothpaste are also considered a liquid. I didn't know that.

Ji-hye: Yeah, they restrict both liquid and gel. Now, shall we go get on our airplane?

So-yeon: Yes! I'm excited. I'm going to shop at the duty-free store.

Ji-hye: So-yeon, I'm sorry but Gimpo Airport's domestic terminal doesn't have a duty-free shop. Don't be so disappointed. There is a duty-free shop at Jeju Airport, so do all the shopping you want on our way back.

Vocabulary

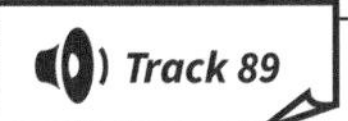

수학여행	school trip
해외여행	overseas trip
(돈을) 모으다	to save up (money)
막상	in the event, when S + is actually about to + V
별 거 없다	to be nothing special
좁다	to be narrow, to be cramped
아쉽다	to be such a pity
길다	to be long
멀다	to be far
나이 먹다	to get old
장시간	long time, long hours
힘들다	to be difficult, to be tough, to be hard
곤욕	trouble, difficulty
액체류	liquid
반입	carrying into
제한	limit
국제선	international flight
용기	container
담기다	to be contained
국내선	domestic flight
대부분	mostly, majority, for the most part
화장품	cosmetics
치약	toothpaste
버리다	to throw away
속하다	to be included, to belong
젤	gel
제한하다	to limit, to restrict
면세점	duty-free shop
실망하다	to be disappointed
마음껏	as much as one likes

Pattern Practice

Study these three grammar patterns that were used in the dialogue and practice!

Pattern I.

처음 VERB + -아/어/여 보는 거예요 formal

This is my first time VERB-ing.

Sentence Used in the Dialogue

저 이번에 비행기 처음 타 보는 거예요.

This is my first time on an airplane.

Sample Sentences

이거 처음 먹어 보는 거예요.

This is my first time eating this.

자동차 처음 사 보는 거예요.

This is my first time buying a car.

Exercises

1. This is my first time listening to this song. (to listen = 듣다, this song = 이 노래)

   ......〉

2. This is my first time doing this exercise. (to do = 하다, this exercise = 이 운동)

   ......〉

Answer Key

1. 이 노래 처음 들어 보는 거예요. *2.* 이 운동 처음 해 보는 거예요.

Applied Patterns

처음 VERB + -아/어/여 봐요

→ 저 이번에 비행기 처음 타 봐요.
This is my first time on an airplane.

*처음 -아/어/여 봐요 is more of a plain statement than the -는 거예요 ending, which is used to "explain" the background.

처음 VERB + -아/어/여요

→ 저 이번에 비행기 처음 타요.
This is my first time on an airplane.

*Even without the verb -보다, since the phrase has 처음, which means "the first time", the meaning mostly stays the same.

Pattern 2.

VERB + -아/어/여 버렸어요 formal

I just ended up VERB-ing. / I just happened to VERB. / (SUBJECT) just PAST TENSE VERB.

Sentence Used in the Dialogue

그 돈으로 물건을 사 버렸어요.

I just ended up buying something with that money.

Sample Sentences

여기까지 와 버렸어요.

I ended up coming all the way here.

치킨을 제 동생이 다 먹어 버렸어요.

My brother just ate all of the chicken.

Exercises

1. The guy just left last month. (to leave = 떠나다, last month = 지난 달)

······〉

2. I just cut that part. (to cut = 자르다, that part = 그 부분)

······〉

Answer Key

1. 그 남자 지난 달에 떠나 버렸어요. *2.* 그 부분 잘라 버렸어요.

Applied Patterns

결국 VERB + -아/어/여 버렸어요

→ 결국 그 돈으로 물건을 사 버렸어요.

I ended up buying something with that money.

Pattern 3.

막상 VERB + -아/어/여 보면 별 거 없어 casual

Actually, when you VERB, there's nothing special.

Sentence Used in the Dialogue

비행기 막상 타 보면 별 거 없어.

Actually, when you are in the airplane, there's nothing special.

Sample Sentences

막상 올라가 보면 별 거 없어.

Actually, if you go up there, there's nothing special.

막상 먹어 보면 별 거 없어.

Actually, when you eat it, it's nothing special.

Exercises

1. Actually, when you meet them, they're nothing special. (to meet = 만나다, them = 그 사람들)

   ......〉

2. Actually, if you go there, there's nothing special. (to go = 가다)

   ......〉

Answer Key

1. 막상 그 사람들 만나 보면 별 거 없어. *2.* 막상 가 보면 별 거 없어.

Applied Patterns

막상 VERB + -아/어/여 보면 별 거 아니야

→ 막상 타 보면 별 거 아니야.

Actually, when you are in the airplane, it's nothing special.

막상 VERB + -아/어/여 보면 아무것도 아니야

→ 막상 타 보면 아무것도 아니야.

Actually, when you are in the airplane, it's just nothing.

Download and listen to the audio track at talktomeinkorean.com/audio.